SCHLOSS IN BAVARIA

THE FASCINATING ROYAL HISTORY OF GERMAN CASTLES

SUSAN SYMONS

Published by Roseland Books
The Old Rectory, St Just-in-Roseland, Truro, Cornwall, TR2 5JD

ISBN 13: 978-0-9928014-6-5
ISBN 10: 099280146X

For Gigi – an adorable force of nature and a bright ray of sunshine.

CONTENTS

1

INTRODUCTION

The year 1791 was an eventful one for Margrave Karl Alexander of Brandenburg-Ansbach. His wife died; he sold his small country and its people to Prussia; then married his mistress and moved with her to England. By the end of the year he was living the leisured life of a British aristocrat on a Prussian pension. This rather shocking story (which I had not heard before) was told to me by the curator when I visited Karl Alexander's palace at Ansbach in northern Bavaria. It's a great example of why the royal history of German castles and palaces is so fascinating. (For more about this story, please see Schloss Ansbach in chapter 2.)

Schloss is the German word for castle or palace and the plural is schlösser. This book visits twenty-five beautiful schlösser in the federal state of Bavaria in Germany and tells some colourful stories about the historical royal characters associated with them. Germany was a monarchy for a thousand years, with a patchwork of different royal states, and these schlösser were an important part of its royal history. When I stood on the shoreline of Lake Starnberg (see Casino, Roseninsel in chapter 6), I could imagine the stormy night-time scene on 13 June 1886, described by a young cook on the royal staff when he helped pull the body of King Ludwig II of Bavaria out of the water[1]. There is still a fierce debate over how the king died.

Bavaria is one of the most beautiful parts of Germany and a great favourite with tourists. I had been to Bavaria several times before, but when I set out with my husband to visit castles and palaces in the state for this book, I was in for some surprises. The federal state is made up of different regions and one surprise was that there is something of a divide between Franconia in the north and the region of Bavaria in the south – this was described to me as being similar to the relationship between Scotland and England! If you think of Bavaria you might conjure up visions of mountains, lederhosen (leather shorts) for men, and the dirndl skirt and apron for women. But that is just the far south, in the region called Bavaria. Franconia, in the north, has its own culture and history and speaks a different dialect of German.

Another surprise was all the royal families I discovered. I associated Bavaria with the glamourous Wittelsbach family, who produced such well-known royal celebrities as Empress Elisabeth of Austria and King Ludwig II of Bavaria. And the Wittelsbacher (collective name for the family) were rulers in Bavaria for nearly seven hundred and fifty years, until the monarchy was abolished in 1918 at the end of World War I. This book tells their enthralling story. But until the early 1800s their rule did not extend to the whole of the present-day federal state. Before then, Franconia and other parts of the state was a kaleidoscope of principalities, church states, and free cities. So, as well as the Wittelsbacher, I found other noble families with fascinating stories I had never heard of before visiting their schlösser.

Appendix A at the back of this book is a map of the federal state of Bavaria – bordered by Austria to the south, the Czech Republic to the east, and other federal states of Germany to the north and west. The map also shows the approximate location of each of the twenty-five schlösser. The book is set out with chapters for the different regions and within each chapter a separate section for each schloss. It starts in the north, at Bamberg in Franconia, and ends in Füssen in the south-west, close to the border with Austria in the region of Swabia. I have tried to include a selection of castles and palaces from different regions and families and also some that are less well-known. Herrenchiemsee (in chapter 6) gets half a million visitors each year and runs tours every few minutes. But at other schlösser we were the only visitors. A reason for writing the book is to encourage more overseas visitors, particularly from the UK and USA, to go and see German schlösser themselves.

Use of the name 'Bavaria'

*The **federal state of Bavaria** is one of the sixteen federal states of Germany and is located in the southeast of the country. It is the largest of the states by land area and the second largest by population.*

*However, things get more complicated because Bavaria is also the name of a region. The federal state of Bavaria is made up of different regions, including the **region of Bavaria** in the southeast of the state (administrative areas of Lower Bavaria and Upper Bavaria). Please see the map in appendix A showing the state and the different regions. The other regions are Franconia (administrative areas of Upper, Lower, and Middle Franconia), Upper Palatinate, and Swabia.*

*History adds another layer of complexity to the use of the name Bavaria because, when Germany was a monarchy, this was also the name of a royal kingdom. What began as the **duchy of Bavaria** in the twelfth century evolved into the **electorate of Bavaria** in the seventeenth, and finally into the **kingdom of Bavaria** in the nineteenth century.*

The word *schloss* can denote different types of royal residence from a fortified castle, to a grand state palace, to a summer villa. The schlösser in this book range in date and style from an eleventh century imperial palace built as a stop-over for the medieval Holy Roman emperors (see Nuremberg in chapter 2); a fifteenth-century stronghold castle where a rich duke kept his treasure chest (Burghausen in chapter 5); an eighteenth century baroque palace to rival Versailles for a prince whose grand ambitions fell apart at the Battle of Blenheim (Schleissheim in chapter 5); to a nineteenth-century holiday home in the Alps for a king and queen who loved hiking (Hohenschwangau in chapter 7).

Another reason for writing the book is to share my view that royal stories from history are fascinating and great fun – more so than any of the adventures of present-day *celebs* in *Hello* magazine. The stories of royal lives from the past can tell us a lot about the times in which they lived, and are as dramatic and action-packed as any story-line from a modern-day soap opera.

The royal stories in this book include the duke whose personal story is so colourful he has been called the Bavarian Henry VIII; the princess who was expected to marry an emperor until he saw her little sister; the king of Bavaria who reigned the longest but who hardly ever appears in the history books because he was insane; and the grandsons of Queen Victoria whose lives went wrong after they were made heir in turn to a German duchy. Appendix C includes charts and family trees to illustrate the royal stories; they are referred to at appropriate points in the text.

I love looking at royal portraits and I even enjoy reading family trees – because both of these help me to fix the historical personalities in my mind and remember their stories. But because the house of Wittelsbach had so many branches over the centuries, their family tree is the most extended and complicated that I have so far tried to get to grips with. During my visits to Bavaria to research this book, I collected as many different genealogical charts for the family as I could lay my hands on, and these were spread out over my dining room table for months. The result is chart 8 in appendix C – my super-simplified version of the Wittelsbach family tree by branch, showing the branches of the house that are mentioned in this book and covering the period from the important division of 1329 up to the present day. Chart 8 is supplemented by charts 9 to 14 which 'zoom in' on particular parts of the Wittelsbacher story. Nearly half (eleven) of the schlösser in this book are associated with this family.

This book looks at the twenty-five schlösser included from two different perspectives. The first perspective is from my observations and impressions when visiting each schloss as part of researching the book. My comments are from the viewpoint of an overseas visitor who does not speak German, and come from my experience at each particular schloss on a particular day. They are entirely personal; another visitor on a different day could have an entirely different experience. The second perspective is given by extracts and stories from the royal history connected with each schloss. The sources I have consulted for this historical information are shown in the notes section and the bibliography at the back of the book. The book is illustrated throughout with a mixture of present-day photographs, old postcards, and royal portraits. This book is not a comprehensive history or detailed travel guide; readers will need to consult the schlösser websites, or other information, for opening hours and directions.

This is my fourth book about the fascinating royal history of German schlösser. Details of the other three are shown at the end of this book and where referred to in the text the titles are shortened for ease to *Schloss, Schloss II, and Schloss III*. I have now been lucky enough to visit nearly one hundred and fifty schlösser in the course of researching my books and a list of all of these is included in appendix B. I hope they might appeal to anyone who likes history or travelogues or who is interested in people's personal stories. I have had a huge amount of fun visiting the schlösser and writing these books.

The most famous castles in the world are in Bavaria. Linderhof, Neuschwanstein, and Herrenchiemsee were all built by Ludwig II, *the Dream King of Bavaria*, as a refuge from dreary reality and his escape into a fantasy world. Ludwig was infected by what another Bavarian prince described as *the devilish building worm*[2], and his obsession for building schlösser, and the resulting parlous state of his finances, was a reason why he was deposed as king. The Bavarian government was desperate to stop the spending. Yet ironically, Ludwig's castles have become a major tourist attraction, and paid for themselves many times over.

The Holy Roman Empire and Bavaria

The Holy Roman Empire of the German Nation was a loose alliance of German and central European states under the leadership of an elected emperor. It had the word 'Roman' in the name because it was considered to be the successor to the Roman empire of the West, that fell to the Barbarians in the fifth century AD; and the word 'Holy' reflected that the early emperors were crowned by the Pope. The Holy Roman Empire existed for nearly a thousand years until, under pressure from Napoleon, it disbanded in 1806.

The Holy Roman Empire was made up of hundreds of independent sovereign territories that were each subject directly to the emperor and the imperial institutions, such as the diet (parliament) and the courts. These territories included secular principalities ruled by a duke or prince, and also ecclesiastical (church) states ruled by the bishop of a diocese or abbot of a monastery. They also included self-governing imperial free cities.

As part of the Holy Roman Empire, there were numerous territories making up the area that is now the federal state of Bavaria. At the turn of the nineteenth century, the largest of these was the Electorate of Bavaria (it was called an electorate because its ruler was a prince-elector – one of a small number of princes who elected the Holy Roman emperor). But there were many others too, particularly in the regions of Franconia and Swabia.

In 1803 the Holy Roman Empire began to break up and most of the church states were dissolved under a process called **secularisation**. Their lands and property were parcelled out among the secular princes in a spectacular land-grab and the elector of Bavaria was a big winner. The elector also proved politically adroit during the Napoleonic Wars (1802-1815), first signing an alliance with Napoleon and then abandoning him when his power waned. So much so that, at the end of the Wars, Bavaria emerged as a kingdom, broadly equivalent in size to today's federal state, that had swallowed up the neighbouring states of the old Holy Roman Empire.

2

FRANCONIA, THE PRINCE-BISHOPS OF BAMBERG AND THE MARGRAVES OF BRANDENBURG-ANSBACH

The region of Franconia did not become part of Bavaria until the start of the nineteenth century when the Holy Roman Empire was broken up during the Napoleonic Wars. Before that Franconia was made up of numerous independent sovereign territories with different ruling structures. These included hereditary principalities such as Brandenburg-Ansbach, ruled by a junior branch of the Hohenzollern family with the rank of margrave (a type of count); church states such as the Bishopric of Bamberg, ruled by an elected prince-bishop; and imperial free cities such as Nuremburg, which was self-governing and not subordinate to any territorial lord or prince.

This chapter includes schlösser from each of these three territories. It visits the imposing palace that went into a time warp after the last ruling prince abdicated and walked away; and the castle of the Holy Roman emperors in the unofficial capital of the Empire. But we start with the schlösser of the prince-bishops of Bamberg, including their grand official residence in Bamberg and a family home in a picturesque area of the countryside called Franconian Switzerland.

New Residence Bamberg

The New Residence on Cathedral Square in Bamberg was built by Lothar Franz von Schönborn, prince-bishop of Bamberg, archbishop-elector of Mainz, and the second highest ranking prince in the Holy Roman Empire after the emperor himself[1]. Lothar Franz was addicted to building and described himself as infected by a worm – the *Teufelsbauwurmb* or devilish building worm[2]. As soon as he was elected prince-bishop of Bamberg in 1693 Lothar Franz began making plans for grand schlösser. But he had to tread carefully because of his election promise not to spend any large sums on building projects. It was only when the Pope ruled two years later (in 1695) that such promises were invalid that he was able to let loose. He extended the Residence

1. The New Residence was the official seat of the prince-bishops of Bamberg.

by building two huge new wings along the side of Cathedral Square working with the architect Leonhard Dientzenhofer. (Leonhard came from a famous family of architects in Franconia and we shall come across them at other schlösser in this chapter.)

The prince-bishops of Bamberg

The prince-bishops of Bamberg were the rulers of a church state in Franconia called the Bishopric of Bamberg (sometimes the Prince-bishopric of Bamberg). The capital of the Bishopric was the city of Bamberg and its territory stretched from the Duchy of Saxe-Coburg and Gotha in the north (see chapter 3) to the imperial free city of Nuremberg in the south (see later in this chapter). At the start of the nineteenth century the Bishopric covered an area of 3,500 square kilometres and had 207,000 inhabitants[3].

The prince-bishops of Bamberg were prelates of the Catholic Church and the spiritual leaders of their diocese. But they were also absolute rulers of a sovereign state, who enjoyed wealth and power and lived in some splendour. Unlike the rulers of a secular state (such as Saxe-Coburg and Gotha), the role of prince-bishop was not hereditary but was elected for life by the Cathedral Chapter or Diocesan authorities. They were highly desirable positions and in practice successful candidates were often the younger sons of great families. In Franconia, the name of one family in particular – the Schönborn – kept coming up.

We were lucky because a quick-thinking curator in the ticket office at Bamberg recognised the chance to add us onto an English tour of the New Residence which was already in progress. We were hurried along to join the group (just two Americans) for the second half of this tour; and then did the first half on our own with the guide. She was a bubbly personality and tremendous fun, filling my head with the colourful characters connected with the schloss. She told us proudly that she had worked at the New Residence for fifteen years and spent more of her time in the schloss than she did at home!

Lothar Franz von Schönborn was a political ally of the Hapsburg Holy Roman emperors and the Kaisersaal (Imperial Hall) on the second floor is his tribute to this Austrian royal house. It is the most ornate and lavishly decorated room in the schloss. Every inch of the walls and ceiling are covered with vibrant and dramatic paintings by the artist Melchior Steidl, including sixteen full-size portraits of the emperors. The hall is only a single story high but Steidl cleverly enhanced the height with trompe l'oeil paintings on the ceiling, so it appears to have two stories and be open to the skies. 'Stand on the star in the middle of the floor' said our guide 'and it feels as if you are looking up to heaven'. 'And see that painted monkey up there clinging to the column? His eyes will follow you all around the room.'

2. Lothar Franz von Schönborn was a passionate builder.

The Imperial Hall leads to a suite of rooms called the Imperial Apartments, installed by Lothar Franz in case a Hapsburg emperor ever made a visit. He never came, but a future empress did. Elisabeth Christine of Brunswick-Wolfenbüttel stayed in the New Residence in 1708, shortly before her marriage to the future Karl VI. To secure this great matrimonial prize she was required to convert to the Catholic faith and Lothar Franz officially accepted her conversion in Bamberg cathedral. Elisabeth Christine's life would be blighted by her failure to produce a male heir, and her husband's attempts to secure the rights of their daughter, Empress Maria Theresa of Austria (the only female Hapsburg ruler), would spark off the War of the Austrian Succession when he died in 1740.

The Schönborn family

Visiting schlösser is always full of surprises and at the New Residence in Bamberg I first heard about the Schönborn family. This important royal dynasty did not have a kingdom or duchy to pass down the family, but instead specialised in being elected as the rulers of church states. As church princes the Schönborn held some of the highest and most powerful positions in the Holy Roman Empire and dominated politics in Franconia between the mid-seventeenth and mid-eighteenth centuries. They were great builders and art collectors, and have left an indelible mark on the culture of Franconia.

Chart 1 shows the three generations of Schönborn who ruled church states in the seventeenth and eighteenth centuries. The story begins when the young Johann Philipp (1605-1673) decided on a spiritual career. He joined the church at a difficult time, during the Thirty Years War that devastated Germany. He proved to be a skilled diplomat and in 1642 was elected as prince-bishop of Würzburg (another church state in Franconia). Church princes could increase their wealth and power by ruling more than one state; in 1647 Johann Philipp was also elected archbishop-elector of Mainz, and in 1663 prince-bishop of Worms. Mainz was the pre-eminent of all the church states, carrying the position of chancellor of the Empire and with the right to crown the Holy Roman emperor.

Johann Philipp was the role model for his nephew, Lothar Franz (1655-1729), who took up the mantle of a great church prince in the next generation. He became prince-bishop of Bamberg in 1693 and two years later also reached the top spot as archbishop-elector of Mainz.

Patronage played an important role in church politics and, in the next generation, four of Lothar Franz's nephews entered the family business and were elected as rulers of six different church states. His favourite nephew, Friedrich Karl (1674-1746), took over as prince-bishop of Bamberg when Lothar Franz died in 1729. Friedrich Karl also hoped to gain the prize of Mainz, but, unlike his uncle and great-uncle who were both shrewd operators, he got on the wrong side of politics and never achieved this.

Beneath the Imperial Apartments are the prince-bishop's own rooms. These are decorated in different styles from across the eighteenth century. The Chinese Cabinet, used to display rare porcelain and lacquer, dates from the time of Lothar Franz at the start of the century, and the cool White Hall, in the classical style, from 1773 and a later prince-bishop. What looks like white marble on the walls in this room is actually polished plaster, using a local technique. For me the charm of the Prince-bishop's Apartments was that the décor is original and had a slightly faded grandeur. The plasterwork in the White Hall showed signs of cracking and the gorgeous yellow silk wallcovering from Lyon in the Yellow Salon had lost its colour. Our guide explained that a major restoration was about to start and these rooms are now closed until 2020. I really hope they won't destroy the charm!

The Bishopric of Bamberg was dissolved in the early nineteenth century, during the secularisation of church states in the Holy Roman Empire, and became part of Bavaria. The schloss was occupied by French troops in the Napoleonic Wars and there was a mysterious death here on 1 June 1815 when Napoleon's much-valued chief of staff, Marshal Berthier, died from a fall out of a window in the Imperial Apartments. He had retired to Bamberg the year before, following Napoleon's first exile to Elba. Why he fell is something of a mystery. The guidebook says it was suicide when Berthier couldn't bear to see Russian troops advancing through the town, but other sources suggest different explanations. One theory is an accident (there was epilepsy in the family so he might have had an attack in front of an open window), another that Berthier was murdered to stop him joining Napoleon at Waterloo (18 June 1815)[4].

After the Napoleonic Wars the schloss became a secondary residence for the kings of Bavaria and this is where King Otto and Queen Amalie of Greece held their Greek court in exile in the 1860s. Otto was the second son of King Ludwig I of Bavaria. As a teenager he was forced to give up his succession rights in Bavaria when his father accepted the throne of Greece (a new country independent of the Ottoman Empire) on his behalf. Otto reigned in Greece for thirty years but never achieved much popularity with his subjects (see Rastede Palais in my second book called *Schloss II* for more of this story). He and his wife, Amalie of Oldenburg, did not have children and Otto struggled to find an heir for Greece. The heir had to be Greek Orthodox and Otto's younger brothers were not keen to convert or to give up their rights in Bavaria.

After he was deposed in a bloodless coup in 1862, Otto and Amalie returned to Bavaria and set up their court in Bamberg. Here they lived out the pretence of still holding the throne – speaking Greek, wearing Greek dress, and surrounded by Greek courtiers. King Otto's private rooms were closed to the public during our visit, but there were large portraits of the couple in the Dining Hall of the Prince-bishop's Apartments, with Otto wearing a Greek outfit. He always hoped to be recalled, but died of the

3. Before Lothar Franz – the Old Bishop's Palace in Bamberg.

measles in 1867. His last wish was to be buried in Greek costume and his last words were 'My Greece, my Greece, my lovely Greece'[5].

In 1900 the Imperial Apartments were refurbished when Prince Rupprecht of Bavaria married Marie Gabrielle, a cousin from another branch of the Wittelsbach family. Rupprecht was third in line to the Bavarian throne and was the grandson of Prince-regent Luitpold, then ruling as regent for the mentally incapacitated King Otto. (Please see chart 12 which has a family tree for the kings of Bavaria). Rupprecht was an army officer stationed at Bamberg and the New Residence became the first home of the newly-weds. Today the rooms are shown as they were when Rupprecht and Marie Gabrielle lived here. They were restored a few years ago using old photographs from 1900.

Rupprecht and Marie Gabrielle were a golden couple; her beauty and high spirits earned her the popular name of *Fairy-tale Queen*[6]. Their first child, Luitpold, was born in the Imperial Apartments in 1901. We saw his cradle – a very posh affair which (our guide suggested) was modelled on that of Napoleon's son, the king of Rome. But the story of their marriage is tragic. In nine years Marie Gabrielle gave birth five times but three of the children died. In 1903 the couple lost their baby daughter Irmingard at six months old from diphtheria, another daughter was stillborn in 1906, and three-year-old Rudolph died from diabetes in 1912.

Marie Gabrielle's health declined and she became depressed. Perhaps Rudolph's death was the last straw; Marie Gabrielle herself died from kidney disease just a few months later, at only thirty-four.

4. Marie Gabrielle of Bavaria with her three sons; she died young and only her middle son survived to adulthood.

More tragedy followed when the eldest child, thirteen-year-old Luitpold, died from polio just after the outbreak of World War I. Rupprecht was on active service and could not attend the funeral[7]. Now Albrecht was his only surviving child. Rupprecht married for a second time after the war and we will come across him, with his second family, at Schloss Berchtesgaden in chapter 6.

After the fall of the German monarchy at the end of World War I, ownership of the New Residence passed to the new Free State of Bavaria. In 1919 it was temporarily the home of the state government (forced out of Munich when a Soviet Republic was declared) and the new state constitution was worked out in the Imperial Hall. Today the schloss is home to a museum of the historic rooms and the Bavarian State Gallery of German and Baroque painting, with a café in the rose garden. The magnificent Imperial Hall can be hired out for events.

Seehof

The guide in Bamberg strongly suggested we should also visit Schloss Seehof at nearby Memmelsdorf, which was the summer palace of the prince-bishops of Bamberg. I have learnt from experience that such recommendations should be heeded. There are thousands of schlösser in Germany and one of the problems is that there is no single list or source to consult in choosing which to visit. Following up local leads has taken us to some of the most fascinating schlösser in my books, including Seehof. This sylvan summer palace is set among green lawns and avenues of trees. The schloss is square-shaped with four symmetrical wings painted mustard yellow and white, around an open courtyard, and a pepper-pot tower in each corner with a grey domed roof. Seehof is a gorgeous-looking schloss and a real success story, because forty years ago it was rescued from a desperate plight.

Three prince-bishops of Bamberg played an important role at Seehof. The first was Marquard Sebastian Schenk von Stauffenberg (reigned 1683-1693), who started the building work in 1687. The schloss is sometimes known as *Marquardsburg* after him. But he died before the work was finished and the schloss was completed by his successor, Lothar Franz von Schönborn (reigned 1693-1729), who was the builder of the New Residence in Bamberg (see above)[8]. Lothar Franz also created the formal baroque garden around the schloss at Seehof. The third prince-bishop was Adam Friedrich von Seinsheim (reigned 1757-1779). He was closely related to the Schönborn family – his mother was the niece of Lothar Franz[9]. Seinsheim redesigned the interior, added four hundred statues around the garden, and built the fabulous water cascade. Seehof was at its most magnificent during his reign.

5. Schloss Seehof is a sylvan summer palace, set among green lawns and avenues of trees.

When the Bishopric of Bamberg was dissolved, Seehof passed to the Wittelsbacher. It was one of many schlösser acquired by the house at this time as Bavaria extended its territory on the break-up of the Holy Roman Empire. Seehof was surplus to requirements and in 1840 it was sold off to the Prussian Colonel von Zandt. It would stay in the ownership of his heirs for the next one hundred and twenty-five years.

The colonel must have been a wealthy man to afford such a palatial home, but over time the money drained away and after World War II his heirs were on their uppers and frantic for cash to keep Seehof going. Starting in 1956 the contents of the schloss were systematically sold off including sculptures, paintings, furniture, and fittings; even the eighteenth-century wallpaper was taken down and sold off by the metre. The schloss was in a terrible state; the roof leaked, the orangeries had become chicken farms, and the gardens turned over to agriculture. Five kilometres of metal pipework carrying water to the cascade in the garden were dug up and sold for scrap. It can't have been easy to wage this war against the odds and the guide told us a sad story about the last von Zandt owners. The last male heir died mysteriously in 1950 by drowning in a shallow pond, leaving a last lady heir as the owner of Seehof. She tried to save the day by marrying a rich man but her strategy misfired. It turned out her new husband thought she was rich because she owned a schloss and would pay his gambling debts[10]! The badly deteriorated schloss was put up for sale and eventually the Free State of Bavaria bought it in 1975. The first thing they did was to fix the roof to stop any further water damage. Forty years later the schloss has been restored and is open to the public during the summer months.

A visit to Seehof starts with a walk through the gardens. Lothar Franz was as passionate about gardens as he was about building and there are still echoes of the formal baroque gardens he created, with different sections (or rooms) bordered by hornbeam hedges and avenues of limes and chestnuts. It took sixteen years (between 1981 and 1997) to restore the amazing water feature built by Prince-bishop von Seinsheim, which had suffered neglect since the bishopric came to an end. The cascade is a series of statues, fountains and water basins running down the hillside behind the schloss. The central figure is a statue of Hercules being crowned with a laurel wreath; on either side of him is a river god. As we arrived at the bottom of the cascade, it sprang into life. Water sprouted from the head of Hercules, poured out of jugs held by the river gods, leaped out of spouts and fountains everywhere, and gushed down between the basins. When the schloss is open the water is turned on for a few minutes every hour, on the hour, and the cascade plays. Wow – what a performance! We would see other fountains on our visits to Bavarian schlösser, but this was the best!

We were the only takers for the guided tour of the Prince-bishop's Apartments and the young guide (who was studying English and history at University) offered to do it in English. What I found so interesting were his snippets of information about how the schloss was restored. The cotton chintz wallpaper in the Writing Cabinet (or study) was recreated from a piece of the 1774 original that had survived, hidden in a blocked-up cupboard behind the desk (the guide opened the cupboard door to show us). The wallcovering in the Bedroom of the First Envoy (main guest bedroom) was reproduced using fragments of material from the original bed canopy which was still at the schloss. It had been badly damaged by water from the leaking roof – presumably the reason why it was not sold off. And in 1992 a team of Chinese artists arrived at Seehof to reconstruct the exquisite green silk wallpaper in the Audience Chamber, sold thirty years before. They worked from a fragile chair covering of the same material. It took a year to hand-paint the new wallpaper, patterned with Chinese motifs of flowers and birds. When they got back to where they started and the last piece of wallpaper joined the first, a small mistake was discovered. There was a slight variation in the shade of the background green colour[11]!

Some of the original furnishings of Seehof are now back in the schloss. The little putti (cherubs) at the top of the staircase are survivors of what were the four hundred statues in the gardens. Pieces of furniture sold in the 1950s have been loaned back by the New York Metropolitan Museum of Art and the chandeliers in the White Hall (banqueting room) were returned in 1989 from Schloss Charlottenburg in Berlin. The ceiling fresco in the rococo White Hall, by the baroque painter Joseph Ignaz Appiani, is the highlight of the tour. It shows a radiant dawn in a luminescent blue sky, surrounded by a ring of the gods – Aurora, goddess of the dawn, the sun god Apollo, Flora (goddess of flowers), Pomona (fruit), Ceres (grain) and Bacchus (wine). The Cupid (messenger of love) in the centre of the ceiling is an optical illusion; wherever you stand in the room, he aims his arrow directly at you. Eighteenth-century paintings often contained an allegory or hidden meaning and this one represents the paradise of life at Seehof during the summer months.

6. Seehof is square-shaped with four pepper-pot towers.

In the eighteenth-century, the rulers of the small German courts wanted to model themselves on the absolute style of monarchy of King Louis XIV of France, and Prince-bishop von Seinsheim tried to create his own (smaller) version of Versailles palace at Seehof. His bedroom (like *the Sun king's* state bedroom in Versailles) is in the centre of the Prince-bishop's Apartments with fine views across the gardens to the cascade and towards the New Residence in Bamberg in the distance. But next to the grand state bed is a more down-to-earth touch – a reproduction of his sleeping chair. Von Seinsheim was a short man who grew so fat that he had to sleep sitting up[12]!

Weissenstein

7. Weissenstein was the private retreat of Lothar Franz von Schönborn.

Schloss Weissenstein at Pommersfelden is a masterpiece of the baroque architectural style and a supreme example of the magnificent court of an eighteenth-century ruler. Prince-bishop of Bamberg Lothar Franz von Schönborn built it later in life and it encompasses all of his talent, passion, and experience as a builder and connoisseur of art. Yet he didn't use it for state purposes or hold his court here. This was his private retreat where he liked to wander the grand rooms that housed his art collection and potter in the garden. Weissenstein was his personal property, as opposed to the New Residence in Bamberg and Schloss Seehof which belonged to the state and were passed on to the next prince-bishop. He left it to his favourite nephew, Friedrich Karl, and it is still owned by the Schönborn family foundation.

Lothar Franz built Weissenstein using a large sum of money he received from the new Holy Roman Emperor Karl VI, when he was elected in 1711. Karl was a Hapsburg and his family enjoyed a monopoly on this position; since 1452 only one emperor had not been a Hapsburg. Nevertheless each Hapsburg candidate had to buy their election with bribes to the nine princes who made up the electoral college. Lothar Franz was one of them and Karl VI paid him the enormous sum of 150,000 guilders in return for his support[13]. He used it to build a new schloss on land he had inherited at Pommersfelden (a village twenty kilometres to the south-west of Bamberg). There was already a moated castle on the site but it was small and old-fashioned and Lothar Franz had it demolished. As a symbolic gesture, the foundation stone for the new schloss was laid on the same day that Lothar Franz (in his role as archbishop-elector of Mainz) crowned Karl VI as Holy Roman emperor in Frankfurt cathedral (1 October 1711). The building work was competed in only seven years (1711-1718) and the payment from the emperor was enough to defray two-thirds of the cost.

The name Weissenstein means white stone and is taken from the colour of the local stone used in the construction. The primary architect was Johann Dientzenhofer (brother of Leonhard who worked on the New Residence at Bamberg) but Lothar Franz himself was very involved in the building design and decoration. The architectural highlight of the schloss is the Central Pavilion which juts out from the main wing and is surmounted by the Schönborn coat-of-arms. This pavilion houses the three great entertaining rooms of the schloss – the Ceremonial Staircase (Treppenhaus), the Marble Hall (Marmorsaal) and the Garden Room (Sala Terrena).

It was three times lucky in a row for us as we enjoyed another personal guided tour in English. It was supposed to be in German but

8. The Ceremonial Staircase (Treppenhaus) where visitors were officially received.

no other visitors turned up and the guide had previously lived in the USA. The tour started on the Ceremonial Staircase which was under renovation and hidden by scaffolding, but our guide gave us a lively description. Twin sets of stairs rise symmetrically on either side of this enormous and elaborately decorated space. They are surrounded by tiers of galleries on all sides, rather like the boxes at a theatre. In a baroque palace the staircase was much more than just a way of getting upstairs; it was where visitors to the court were ceremonially received. An audience of courtiers would watch the performance from the galleries and could judge the rank and importance of each guest by where on the staircase they were officially greeted and by whom. If the emperor had ever come to Weissenstein (he didn't), even Lothar Franz would have descended the stairs to meet him.

The staircase leads into the Marble Hall intended for use on state occasions. This is huge (twenty-one metres long, fourteen metres wide, and fifteen metres high) and takes its name from the marble used for the floor and the lower part of the columns around the walls. The upper part is imitation marble (not for reasons of cost, but to reduce the weight of the room). Lothar Franz put up portraits of Emperor Karl VI and his wife Elizabeth Christine in this room, but when the emperor never came to visit he took these down and hung Schönborn family portraits instead.

Beneath the Marble Hall is the Sala Terrena or Garden Hall with thick walls and vaulted ceilings to support the weight of all that marble above it. This is one of the strangest-looking rooms and is decorated as a grotto or underground fairy-kingdom. The walls and ceiling are covered with little pieces of coloured stone and glass, semi-precious gems, slivers of mirror, and sea shells. There are icicles of crystal glass and everything is frosted with flakes of white mica, so that one writer said this

...creates a fairy-tale vision in which snow and cold seem to have engulfed the decoration...[14]

It must have looked magical by candlelight, when everything glistened and glittered. Weissenstein was a summer palace and the Garden Hall was designed to stay cool – it was a warm day outside but the temperature in here was a chilly ten degrees.

I found it ironic that Lothar Franz designed such a fabulous entertaining suite as these three rooms and then never used it. The guide told us there were no balls or big parties here in his day. However, every summer now these rooms are full with audiences who come to hear the concerts given by young musicians from around the world as part of the annual music academy, held at Weissenstein since 1958.

9. The Central Pavilion (on the left) is the architectural highlight
of Weissenstein.

Lothar Franz was a passionate collector of paintings who commissioned many original works and also employed agents to search out paintings to buy. In his lifetime he amassed a collection of two thousand paintings and wrote proudly to his nephew Friedrich Karl that 'Only the imperial gallery [of the Holy Roman emperor] and the gallery of the elector of the Palatine can compare with mine[15]. He designed the layout of Weissenstein so that his own apartments were one side of the Central Pavilion and the guest rooms on the other.

The Great Gallery for his paintings was (of course) on his side of the building. Later generations of Schönborn had to sell some of the collection, but there are still six hundred of Lothar Franz's paintings at Weissenstein, including Dürer, Titian, Brueghel, Rubens, and Van Dyck. It is one of the largest private collections in Germany. There are paintings in every room on the tour, hung cheek by jowl. Our guide told us the schloss has its own micro-climate which helps to preserve them. Weissenstein is also still home to the library of precious books and manuscripts collected by Lothar Franz, but this is not open to the public.

Prince-bishop Lothar Franz von Schönborn was a cultured and talented prince and Weissenstein is his crowning achievement. It has been carefully preserved by the Schönborn family right up until today. He was also a good businessman who founded the family fortune. The story goes that Lothar Franz owned ninety-eight properties and was very careful not to increase this number. This was because, should it reach one hundred, he would have to pay a special tax to the Holy Roman emperor[16]! Lothar Franz is still very present in his schloss because much of what the visitor sees is original and there is a portrait or bust of him, or his initials, in every room.

The Castle Road

Die Burgenstrasse or the Castle Road is a tourist route which stretches for 1200 kilometres between Mannheim in south-west Germany (south of Frankfurt) and Prague in the Czech Republic. It passes more than ninety castles and palaces, which are shown in the marketing brochure and on the website (www.burgenstrasse.de which has English translation). The route sweeps through Franconia, and several of the schlösser in this book are on the Castle Road. In the order of the book they are

Bamberg ✷ Seehof ✷ Greifenstein ✷ Forchheim ✷ Nuremberg ✷ Ansbach ✷ Coburg – Ehrenburg, Veste Coburg, Callenberg

Greifenstein

The area of Franconia known as *Franconian Switzerland* was given this name in the nineteenth century because the picturesque scenery reminded artists and poets of Switzerland. What a pity the sun isn't shining, everyone said, so you are not seeing Franconian Switzerland at its best. But I loved it just as we did see it, on an overcast and rainy day, with drifts of mist on the mountains and drizzle in the damp lush valleys. The bumpy side road looped through neat half-timbered villages and it seemed as if there was a castle on every hill-top – Egloffstein, Gössweinstein, Pottenstein ... and others. Our destination was Schloss Greifenstein (or stone stronghold) near the village of Heiligenstadt.

10. Greifenstein in Franconian Switzerland has been in the ownership of the Stauffenberg family since 1691.

It was still raining when we got there to find a small group outside the schloss, huddled under their umbrellas in front of closed doors and a notice saying a tour would start in half an hour. It looked as if they were going to wait it out where they were, but we followed a nearby path and happily found a beer garden where we passed the time in cosy comfort. Just after the scheduled start time a head popped round the door and seemed surprised to find anyone outside. Our guide had arrived and the tour began. There was no material in English (English-speaking visitors are rare here), and we were not allowed to take photos. But I still had a wonderful time. Schloss Greifenstein has been owned by the same family for over three hundred years and is packed full of interesting contents. Our guide was both knowledgeable and passionate and she made this a memorable visit. The tour was due to take forty minutes but lasted for an hour and a half!

There has been a castle at Greifenstein since at least the twelfth century; the first documented mention was in 1172. When the previous owners died out in 1690, the old castle reverted to the Bishopric of Bamberg and in 1691 it was given to the then prince-bishop, Marquard Sebastian Schenk von Stauffenberg. Before his death two years later, the prince-bishop transformed the old medieval castle into a four-wing baroque palace with the help of the Bamberg court architect Leonhard Dientzenhofer. Both these names are already familiar – Stauffenberg was also the builder of Schloss Seehof and Leonhard Dientzenhofer went on to build the New Residence at Bamberg with Stauffenberg's successor, Lothar Franz von Schönborn.

The Stauffenberg family can also trace their roots back to the early twelfth century. The present head of house and owner of Greifenstein is Christoph Schenk Graf von Stauffenberg, born in 1950. The family name is unusual because it includes both a hereditary title (schenk or cupbearer) which comes first, followed by the hereditary rank (graf or count). Graf Christoph and all living members of the family are descended from Adam Friedrich (1767-1808). In 1874 his son, Franz Ludwig (1801-1881), was promoted from freiherr (baron) to graf (count) by King Ludwig II of Bavaria. Please see chart 2 for a family tree.

What is appealing is that Greifenstein is a delightful mix of museum and family home. As we entered the schloss at the start of the tour I noticed a gentle aroma – hard to describe, but rather pleasant. 'Old castle' murmured my husband as he sniffed appreciatively. The first rooms are the armoury in the south wing, housing a notable collection which traces the development of weapons from the sword to the repeating gun. There is so much to see that I wished I could follow more of the German commentary. In a lively performance our guide demonstrated several of the exhibits, including rifles, a World War I gasmask, and a basket for the carrier pigeons who delivered military messages. She also showed us an intriguing iron chain with a ball that split into two and fitted back again. I have still not discovered the purpose of this.

Then back into the pretty inner courtyard which has walls painted cream, grey doors and windows, and pink casuarina trees in pots. The well in the corner is so deep that it took over ten seconds for the contents of a glass of water (poured down the well by our guide) to hit the water at the bottom. An imposing doorway in the centre of the west wing, surmounted by the Stauffenberg coat of arms, leads to the schloss chapel. The Latin inscription over the door is both a line of verse and a date (this

11. A Latin inscription over the door to the chapel is a *Chronostichon* – both a line of verse and a date.

is called a *Chronostichon*). The verse translates as 'The power comes from God and heals all' and the date is 1723, the year the chapel was sanctified[17]. Inside the chapel we sat in the pews while the guide talked about a group photograph of the previous count and his family. Graf Otto-Philipp (the father of Christoph) moved into Greifenstein in 1949 and lived here for sixty-five years until his death in 2015.

On the first floor, above the chapel, is the Ancestral Hall. The stunning long room has beautiful patterned floorboards and an amazing

12. The Ancestral Hall with amazing marquetry and heraldic discs showing the coats of arms of the Stauffenberg ladies.

marquetry cabinet at the far end which, our guide said, took one man forty years to make. The walls are hung with heraldic discs showing the coats of arms of the ladies who married into the Stauffenberg family over the centuries. The latest is dated 1987 when Graf Christoph married Gräfin Monika Reichserbtruchsessin von Waldburg zu Zeil und Trauchburg[18].

My favourite rooms in the schloss are on the first floor in the north wing. I love books and walking into the Library took my breath away! There are five thousand volumes here and our guide donned a pair of white cotton gloves to turn the pages of an old book called *The Chronicle of Nuremberg*, dating from the early sixteen hundreds. I especially liked that new books are still being added to the library – on the next shelf was a paperback John Le Carre! It's a well-used room, cluttered with family memorabilia. A small glass-fronted cabinet contained the three Stauffenberg family wedding crowns – one each for the wedding, silver and golden anniversaries. The feeling of a home was emphasised by the sound of someone practising on the piano in the room next door.

The last room on the tour (the Jagdzimmer or Hunting Room) was thought-provoking because it has a memorial to the most famous family member – Oberst (colonel) Claus Schenk Graf von Stauffenberg, the disillusioned war veteran who tried to assassinate Hitler and trigger a military coup by planting a bomb in East Prussian headquarters on 20 July 1944. The bomb exploded and several died, but Hitler escaped with minor injury. Claus was summarily shot the same night but his elder brother, Berthold, was tortured and suffered a lingering death, being executed with great cruelty three weeks later. Hitler wanted vengeance on the entire family. On 21 July, Greifenstein was occupied by the Gestapo and Claus's elderly uncle, eighty-five year old Graf Berthold, head of the family and owner of the schloss, was arrested. He died a few months later following his ill-treatment[19]. His portrait hangs by the photo and bust of Claus in the Jagdzimmer. Claus's pregnant wife was also arrested and imprisoned and their four children sent to a children's home and given different names[20].

13. The Trophies Corridor in the north wing.

After the war they were reunited and today the Stauffenberg family has over a hundred members, scattered around the world.

Kaiserpfalz Forchheim

Almost the first thing we discovered when we visited this schloss is that, despite its name, it is not in fact a kaiserpfalz, or imperial palace. In the middle ages the Holy Roman emperor travelled constantly and there were many imperial palaces scattered around the Empire to provide accommodation for him and his retinue (including Nuremberg – see below). There was a kaiserpfalz at Forchheim and until recently it was believed to have been on the site of the schloss. Although that is now thought unlikely, the name has stuck.

Kaiserpfalz Forchheim was a secondary residence for the prince-bishops of Bamberg.

The town of Forchheim was at the southern end of the Bishopric of Bamberg and Kaiserpfalz Forchheim was built by Prince-bishop Lambert von Brunn (reigned 1374-1399) as a secondary residence. By the time the church state was dissolved in 1803 (and Forchheim became part of Bavaria) the fortunes of the Kaiserpfalz had long been in decline. During the nineteenth century it was used as a tobacco store, offices, apartments and a police station. But when rumours began to circulate at the start of the twentieth century, that the State of Bavaria was planning to demolish the schloss or alternatively turn it into a lunatic asylum, the residents of Forchheim were shocked. They banded together to save it and a preservation society was formed; the first museum opened in 1911.

Today Kaiserpfalz Forchheim is owned by the town and is home to several museums and a cultural centre. I really liked the imaginative way in which new design has been combined with preservation of the old to make this historic building fit for purpose today. At the rear is a dramatic glass tower with a new staircase and lift to the upper floors. We received a very warm welcome from the lady on the reception desk who was determined that we should enjoy our visit. They don't get many English visitors here, but after scrabbling around in the drawers she found an English audio-guide tucked away. Most visitors headed for the Archaeological Museum on the lower floors. This holds the biggest treasure of the schloss – the fragments of its medieval wall paintings that have survived, some of which date from the original decorations commissioned by Prince-bishop Lambert von Brunn. But what I most enjoyed was the Town Museum on the top floor about the history of Forchheim. No other visitors got this far and we were on our own up there!

This museum explores the eight-hundred-year history of the Bishopric of Bamberg, from its foundation in 1007 to dissolution in 1803. To my delight it had portraits of the prince-bishops, including Lambert von Brunn and the others in this chapter. Over centuries the prince-bishops built a complex ring of fortifications around the town to help defend the southern boundary of their state. Kaiserpfalz Forchheim was besieged several times during the Thirty Years War (1618-1648) but never taken.

The museum has old prints and maps of the town and a beautiful set of watercolours by local painter Michael Kotz (1848-1915) giving an artist's impression of different parts of the fortifications. There is also a large model on which visitors can press buttons to illuminate different lights and find out which parts of the fortifications were built when and by which prince-bishop. Apart from the Kaiserpfalz, the only part still standing today is the Nuremberg Tower, built by Lothar Franz von Schönborn in 1698.

A dramatic glass tower combines new design with preservation of the old.

Kaiserburg Nuremberg

The best way to get to the Kaiserburg in Nuremberg is to walk through Altstadt (the historic old walled city). The schloss is built on Castle Rock in the north-east section of the wall and dominates the skyline of the old city. On our way there we passed many of the other historic sights – including the Gothic church of St Lorenz and the Rathaus (town hall). As we toiled up the hill, Kaiserburg Nuremberg towered above us, its buildings strung out in a long line.

14. The Kaiserburg towers above the historic old walled city of Nuremberg.

In the middle ages the Imperial Free City of Nuremberg was one of the most important centres in the Holy Roman Empire and has been called its unofficial capital. Medieval emperors did not have any permanent residence where they held court and Nuremberg was a regular stopping place for these itinerant rulers as they travelled the empire. There were many imperial palaces scattered around their territory including Kaiserburg Nuremberg and Kaiserpfalz Forchheim (see above). The emperors favoured Nuremberg because of its central location and also because it was neutral ground and not under the dominion of any prince. For five hundred years, from its foundation around 1050, all of the emperors stayed in the schloss. One of the most famous was Friedrich I (known as Barbarossa or red-beard) who resided in Nuremberg regularly during his long reign (1152-1190). His last visit was in 1188, when he received the ambassadors of the Byzantine Empire. Friedrich left on Crusade the following year and never returned; he drowned attempting to cross a river.

Karl IV (reigned 1347-1378) treated Nuremberg as a second home (to Prague where he was born); he stayed here a total of fifty-two times and built the beautiful Frauenkirche (Church of Our Lady) in the city. The official assembly (called an imperial diet) convened by Karl IV at Nuremberg in 1356 issued a key document in the history of the empire called the *Golden Bull* which regulated the process for electing an emperor. This stipulated that each new emperor must hold his first imperial diet in Nuremberg. The pre-eminence of Nuremberg was confirmed during the reign of Emperor Sigismund when the imperial insignia, used at the coronation of the emperors, were brought to the city in 1424 for safekeeping. They remained in Nuremburg until the dying days of the Holy Roman Empire when the last emperor (a Hapsburg) took them back to Vienna.

There were a lot of visitors at the Kaiserburg; it was by far the busiest place we had been so far. We spent a long time at the schloss and most of it was in the double imperial chapel and double imperial hall.

15. Entrance to the Kaiserburg; the tower in the centre houses the double imperial chapel.

The Burgraves' Castle

The first thing we stumbled across when we arrived at the Kaiserburg, was the story of a different castle altogether. The Burgraves' Castle was built next door to the imperial palace, and we walked past what remains of it on our way in. This castle, which burned down in 1420, is part of the history of the Hohenzollern family, who began their rise as burgraves of Nuremberg before becoming electors of Brandenburg, kings of Prussia, and finally kaisers (emperors) of Germany. But here in Nuremberg the citizens carried on a feud with the Hohenzollern family and eventually drove them out!

The burgrave of Nuremberg was the hereditary governor of the Kaiserburg. In 1192, Friedrich III of Hohenzollern succeeded his father-in-law and became Burgrave Friedrich I of Nuremberg. Friedrich had married the daughter of the last of the previous line of burgraves (the Grafs von Raabs). From their seat in the Burgraves' Castle the Hohenzollerns went on to build up considerable lands in Franconia but they also increasingly came into conflict with the wealthy city of Nuremberg.

As an imperial free city (from 1219), Nuremberg had self-governing rights and was subject directly to the emperor. The city did not relish having these ambitious local lords on the doorstep and so they set about freezing them out. In 1367 the city built a huge wall in front of the Burgraves' Castle to barricade it in, and ten years later they erected a tall watchtower (called the Luginsland) smack bang next to it to spy in. The burgrave complained to the emperor that his rights were being infringed but there was no response. In the 1380s armed citizens of Nuremberg occupied the Burgraves' Castle by force and when it burned down in 1420 there was suspicion that the gates were opened to let the attackers in. The Hohenzollerns had now had enough; they sold the ruins of the Burgraves' Castle to the city and left Nuremberg.

Their power base had already moved away when, in 1415, the Hohenzollerns became electors of Brandenburg in the north east of the Holy Roman Empire. But they held onto their lands in Franconia, as a foothold in southern Germany, and these were later split into the two principalities of Brandenburg-Ansbach and Brandenburg-Bayreuth.

Entrance to the double imperial chapel and double imperial hall is from the inner courtyard, where the Kunigunde Lime Tree grows in the centre. Legend has it that there has been a lime tree on this spot for a thousand years, since the first one was planted by St Kunigunde, the wife of Emperor Heinrich II. It is not the same tree of course and has been replaced several times in the twentieth century. Guided tours were available but only in German, so we did a self-guided tour using the English guidebook, which is detailed and comprehensive. When I asked about a plan of the buildings the curator gallantly presented me with a free copy of the old guidebook, that has one at the back.

The double imperial chapel is a double-decker with two chapels on the same floor plan, one above the other. There is no staircase or direct access between the two, but a large rectangular opening in the floor/ceiling allowed the congregation in one chapel to hear the service in the other. Visitors see the upper chapel and can look down through the opening to the lower chapel below. Scholars are uncertain of the precise date that the Nuremberg double chapel was built, but it certainly dates back to 1216 when the lower chapel was given to the Teutonic Order[21]. The upper chapel was used by the court and has a gallery (a third level reached by a staircase in the wall), reserved for the emperor and his family. At one end of this is a small and gloomy cabin partitioned off in 1520 for Karl V as a private oratory (place of worship) [22].

The floor area is small but the upper chapel is lofty and serene, with four slender, tall columns (one in each corner of the opening) supporting the vaulted ceiling. I would have much preferred to worship here than in the dark and cramped oratory. I liked the sense of history with all the events that must have happened in this chapel. In 1431 Prince Vlad of Wallachia was invested here with the Order of the Dragon by Emperor Sigismund, in reward for his bravery and helping to protect the eastern boundary of the Empire against the Turks. Thereafter he was known as Vlad Dracul (dracul means dragon), and his son was the historical figure on which Bram Stoker based his thrilling novel *Dracula* [23]!

The double imperial hall is also a double-decker with two large reception rooms on the same floorplan; the Emperor's Hall on the upper level, above the Knights' Hall. There was a tragic accident here in 1225 when the staircase between these two halls collapsed and a large number of people were killed. They were guests at the castle for the important wedding of the emperor's son to an Austrian Hapsburg. But the festivities got mixed up with a trial after a guest was murdered on his way to the wedding. During a dispute about how to punish the murder, the staircase became overcrowded with spectators and broke apart.

16. An old picture of the inner courtyard at the Kaiserburg with the entrance to the double imperial hall.

I am interested in the history of the Holy Roman Empire and have long bemoaned that there are so few books in English on this subject. (The recent masterful and scholarly tome by Peter Wilson is a great addition to the literature.[24]) So it was a lovely surprise to find an exhibition devoted to the Holy Roman Empire in the Emperor's Hall. Around the room were a number of interactive visitor stations, addressing different questions such as 'Who selected the head of Empire?' and 'How did the emperor ensure the loyalty of his subjects?'. The answers were spiced with examples and illustrated lavishly, and (joy of joys) everything was translated into English! I looked at pictures of the crown of Charlemagne and the seal of Friedrich Barbarossa; I read the stirring tale of the throne dispute which followed the death of Heinrich VI in 1197. Two factions each chose a rival emperor from different powerful families and the position was very confused. One of these emperors (Philipp of Swabia) was murdered (in Bamberg by a Wittelsbach) and the other (Otto IV) was excommunicated by the pope. Eventually things were resolved by the election of Friedrich II (the son of Heinrich VI) at an imperial diet in Nuremberg in 1211.

I was totally absorbed by this fascinating exhibition. Guided tour after guided tour passed through the Emperor's Hall but I was still there, eagerly pressing buttons and soaking up the answers. Only the need for food and drink eventually dragged me away.

Ansbach

The schloss at Ansbach was the main residence of the margraves of Brandenburg-Ansbach (a margrave or margraf is a variation on the title of graf, or count). It is a large and imposing building but curiously cut off from the town by a major road on three sides, so that it felt as if the schloss was on a traffic island! As we toured the state rooms, all I could see from the windows was the road, with no sign of a schloss garden anywhere. I discovered later that there is one (the very beautiful Hofgarten – see below) but it is some distance away, out of sight, on the other side of the road.

What is special at Ansbach is that the state rooms of the schloss have hardly been touched since the last margrave left in 1791 and the schloss went into a time warp! The guided tour visits three sets of apartments on the first floor that make up the state rooms and were used for formal occasions – the Margrave's Apartments, the Margravine's Apartments (his wife's) and the Guest Apartments. These magnificent rooms were mostly decorated between 1734 and 1745 for the last margrave but one, Karl Wilhelm Friedrich, using the money from his wife's dowry.

He married a sister of Frederick the Great of Prussia. The tour goes through twenty-seven rooms around all four wings of the schloss, and we saw one gorgeous interior after another. I particularly remember two sumptuous small rooms between the margrave's and his wife's apartments, called the Mirror and the Marble Cabinets, where only very special guests would be invited.

17. The schloss at Ansbach was the residence of
the margraves of Brandenburg-Ansbach.

The Mirror Cabinet was the most expensive room in the schloss because mirrors were difficult to produce and very costly to buy in the eighteenth century[25]. The walls are panelled with mirrors and embellished by extravagantly ornate gilding. The golden frames around the mirrors incorporate niches and plinths for a collection of one hundred and sixty-six delicate Meissen porcelain figures, dating from 1740-1760. The effect of all this mirrored glass, gold, and china, in a small space, quite assaults the senses! The walls of the Marble Cabinet are lined with pink and grey stucco (this is imitation and not real marble), but what I found intriguing was the subject of the six paintings. They illustrate the vices (an unusual subject for a palace) showing greed, lust, pride, sloth, cruelty and wastefulness. The picture illustrating greed was of a group of men gloating over a big pile of coins.

The margraves of Brandenburg-Ansbach and Brandenburg-Bayreuth

Brandenburg-Ansbach and Brandenburg-Bayreuth were small principalities in Franconia, each belonging to a junior branch of the Hohenzollern family. By the decree of Elector Albrecht Achilles of Brandenburg in 1473, the Hohenzollern family lands were divided into three – the electorate of Brandenburg (the senior branch of the family) and the margraviates of Brandenburg-Ansbach and Brandenburg-Bayreuth. The senior branch was promoted to kings of Prussia in 1701 and kaisers of Germany in 1871.

The line of Brandenburg-Bayreuth came to an end in 1769 on the death of Margrave Friedrich Christian (1708-1769). By family agreement Brandenburg-Bayreuth then passed to his third cousin twice removed, Margrave Karl Alexander of Brandenburg-Ansbach (1736-1806). Please see chart 3 for a family tree. But Karl Alexander was also the last man standing in his branch of the family (he had no heir) and unless he had children (which seemed unlikely), both junior branches would be extinct on his death.

Karl Alexander pre-empted the situation when, in 1791, he abdicated his rights and sold both Brandenburg-Ansbach and Brandenburg-Bayreuth to the senior branch of the Hohenzollern family in Prussia. During the Napoleonic Wars each principality was ceded by Prussia to France before ending up, by the end of the wars, as part of the new kingdom of Bavaria.

There was a handout in English for the (German) guided tour and this was helpful on the layout and décor of the rooms. But it had nothing about the portraits or the history of the family – how frustrating was that! For me portraits are an important part of any schloss visit and knowing something about the history of the family can bring the place to life. The tour stopped for a long time while our guide told what, judging by the reaction of fellow visitors, was an interesting story. My husband speaks some German but this was too fast for him to follow.

'It seems to be about the last margrave', he told me, 'I think it's a love tangle!'. The guide was kind and after the tour we sat in the Gothic Hall where, in between manning the museum shop, she told me the story of the last margrave and the three ladies in his love tangle – his wife and two mistresses. I think this is as good as any plot in a modern-day TV drama!

The last margrave of Brandenburg-Ansbach was Karl Alexander,

born in 1736. He was the son of Karl Wilhem Friedrich who redecorated the state rooms with his wife's dowry. When he was eighteen Karl Alexander was married off to Friederike Caroline of Saxe-Coburg-Saalfeld. It was an arranged marriage and a complete flop. The couple were not in love, had little in common, and did not have any children. The suggestion is this was the fault of Karl Alexander who suffered from venereal disease before the marriage which made

18. Entrance to the beautiful baroque Hofgarten (Court Garden).

him sterile[26]. He would have two wives and several mistresses but, so far as is known, never any children.

Friederike Caroline did claim to be pregnant the year after their marriage but too many months went by and the pregnancy was false. (The guide at Ansbach suggested she faked it to avoid her husband's attentions.) After that they lived separate lives; Karl Alexander took little notice of his wife and Friederike Caroline became an invalid (she suffered from tuberculosis), querulous, and pious[27]. The margrave's subjects may have wondered why he did not divorce her and marry again to secure the succession. But perhaps he knew it would be pointless as he could not father children. He travelled widely and he kept mistresses. The two mistresses in his love tangle were both famous women in their own right.

The first on the scene was Hippolyte Clairon (known as *La Clairon*) the leading French actress of her day who had worked with Voltaire at the Comédie Française. She was nearly fifty and retired from the stage when Karl Alexander asked her to relocate from Paris to Ansbach as his official mistress in 1772. Their arrangement worked well for fifteen years – *La Clairon* graced the society of Ansbach, her retirement was funded in luxury by

19. The famous French actress, *La Clairon*, was the official mistress of Margrave Karl Alexander.

the margrave's state revenues, and she did not interfere in politics. But then the villain in the piece turned up.

Lady Elizabeth Craven was an English aristocrat, playwright, and travel writer, who was notorious for her scandalous lifestyle and had left behind a husband, five children, and numerous lovers when she arrived in Ansbach in 1787, at the invitation of Karl Alexander. She was much younger than her rival (in her late thirties), and much more ruthless. She wasted no time in ousting La Clairon and for the next few years Lady Craven lorded it as the favourite in Ansbach, where she made herself very unpopular. Karl Alexander was besotted – apparently he liked bossy women[28]!

For Lady Craven her new relationship must have seemed a golden opportunity. The margrave was handsome (he was called 'the most handsome man in Franconia'[29]), cultured, rich, and royal. For her, Ansbach had no allure in comparison to living in London and she persuaded Karl Alexander that, because he had no heir, he need not worry about his principality – far better to pass over his responsibilities now, and enjoy life. For the king of Prussia, the little state of Brandenburg-Ansbach was a strategically important outpost in southern Germany to counter the power block of Austria. So Karl Alexander negotiated the sale of his country and its people to Prussia in return for a very large annual pension. Early in 1791 he abdicated his rights and left Ansbach[30]. By a stroke of fortune (that even Lady Craven could not have engineered) both Karl Alexander's wife and Lady Craven's husband died that same year, and Lady Craven and the margrave were married on 13 October 1791. Her friend, the English politician Horace Walpole, wrote in his correspondence

Lady Craven received the news of her Lord's death on a Friday, went into weeds on Saturday, and into white satin and *many* diamonds on Sunday, and in that vestal trim was married to the Margrave of Anspach[31].

Karl Alexander and his second wife moved to England where they lived between Brandenburg House at Fulham in London and a country seat at Benham Park, near Newbury in Berkshire. (This had been Lady Craven's country home with her first husband and Karl Alexander bought it from Lord Craven's family.) But according to the guide at Ansbach, there was no happy ending to the story. La Clairon returned to Paris where she died in poverty in 1803. Lady Craven was a bad wife who did not change her flighty ways and the last margrave always regretted not sticking with his French lady. 'La Clairon cost him money but Lady Craven cost him his country.' The last margrave of Brandenburg-Ansbach died at Benham Park in 1806.

At the end of our visit we took a stroll through the beautiful Hofgarten (Court Garden), on the other side of the busy road. This formal baroque garden was originally laid out by Karl Alexander's grandmother and rebuilt after being badly damaged in World War II. I am a keen gardener and this is the style of garden I like best, with formal paths, neat lawns, topiary, and colourful flower beds.

The centrepiece is an elegant orangery, over one hundred metres long, which now houses a restaurant and café. It was a public holiday and the Hofgarten was humming with families out enjoying the sunshine; it was far busier here than at the schloss. But in a quiet spinney away from the main parterre we found a surprise – a memorial to the mysterious Kaspar Hauser, who was mortally stabbed in the Ansbach Hofgarten on 14 December, 1833.

The identity of Kaspar Hauser is one of those intriguing mysteries that captured the public imagination. In 1828 an unknown youth turned up in Nuremberg where he tried to enlist in the cavalry. He could write his name (Kaspar Hauser) but knew nothing about his background and claimed to have been kept in a cell for much of his life and fed on bread and water. (This was clearly not true as he appeared to be well-nourished.[32]) There was much speculation about the identity of this strange boy and he became a celebrity. Soon the idea was circulating that he was a lost prince – the rightful ruler of the

20. The mysterious Kaspar Hauser – was he a lost royal prince?

Grand Duchy of Baden. According to this story Kaspar was the son and heir of Grand Duke Karl of Baden and had been snatched as a new-born, to take him out of the succession, with a sickly baby substituted who died soon after.

The Baden story seems unlikely but Kaspar's real identity has never been established. Some people said he was an attention seeker who may have stabbed himself. But if his dying words are to be believed, Kaspar Hauser was attacked in the Ansbach Hofgarten by an unknown assailant and his murder has never been solved.

Caroline of Ansbach

Much to my surprise, I could not find any trace at Ansbach of Queen Caroline of Great Britain (the wife of George II). Caroline was born a princess of Brandenburg-Ansbach and is always known in British history as 'Caroline of Ansbach'. But there was no portrait of Caroline at the schloss and the guide knew nothing about her. This is because, although born in Ansbach in 1683, Caroline spent little time here during her life.

Caroline was the daughter of Margrave Johann Friedrich of Brandenburg-Ansbach. Her mother was the margrave's second wife and did not get on with his family; so when Johann Friedrich died of smallpox in 1686, his widow moved away. Caroline was brought up first at Eisenach (her mother's home), then in Saxony during her mother's disastrous second marriage to the elector of Saxony (see Rochlitz in 'Schloss' for this story), and then (after her mother's death in 1696) as a ward at the Brandenburg court.

In 1705 Caroline married Prince George Augustus of Hannover who was third in line to the British throne after his grandmother (Electress Sophia of Hannover) and his father (later George I). She was queen consort of Great Britain from her husband's accession as George II in 1727 until her own death in 1737.

3

FRANCONIA
AND THE DUKES OF
SAXE-COBURG AND GOTHA

If you are interested in royal history you should visit the town of Coburg in Upper Franconia. This was the home of one of Europe's most important dynasties, whose rise up the royal ranks is such an extraordinary story. At the start of the nineteenth century the Coburg family were the rulers of a small German duchy; a century later they sat on a dozen European thrones including that of Great Britain. This chapter visits the schlösser where Queen Victoria's parents were married and where her beloved husband Albert was born; but also discovers how inheriting Coburg was a poisoned chalice for her British grandsons, and meant they were on the opposite side to the rest of the family during World War I.

It was market day in Coburg and later on the streets would be throbbing, with the statue of Prince Albert obscured by the paraphernalia of market stalls. But when we arrived first thing in the morning there was no-one about and we had the Schloss-platz (Palace Square) to ourselves. The damp, overcast skies gave Ehrenburg an almost ethereal look. In my experience you need to start early to see schlösser at their best.

Ehrenburg

In 1543 Duke Johann Ernst decided to transfer his court from the old fortress at Coburg (Veste Coburg – see later in this chapter) to a palace in the town and work began to convert an abandoned and dilapidated Franciscan monastery. It is thought that the name Ehrenburg (Honourable Castle) was given to the new schloss by the Holy Roman Emperor (Karl V) who was a guest of the duke here soon after it was completed in 1547[1]. Later dukes extended the schloss and, after a disastrous fire on 9 March 1690, it was remodelled in baroque style by Duke Albrecht. But Ehrenburg owes its appearance today largely to the father of Prince Albert – who was Duke Ernst I of Saxe-Coburg and Gotha (1784-1844)[2].

When Ernst I inherited his duchy in 1806, its finances were in a precarious state. But he had a vision for the modernisation of Ehrenburg so he set up a building fund and hired a good architect to make drawings[3]. Over the next thirty years, working on a stop-go basis (as and when

21. Ehrenburg was the home of one of Europe's most important
royal dynasties.

funds were available), Ernst I added new neo-gothic facades to the building and refurbished the interiors in French empire style, bringing furniture, clocks and chandeliers from Paris. His last big project was to clear away the old houses crowding around the schloss to create a vast and new Schloss-platz with sweeping views up through a hillside park to the old fortress. The raised terrace called the Arcades, where we stood to take photos, had only just been completed when Ernst I's daughter-in-law, Queen Victoria, visited Coburg for the first time in August 1845.

22. Statue of Duke Ernst I outside Ehrenburg.

Queen Victoria (1819-1901) married Prince Albert of Saxe-Coburg and Gotha (1819-1861), the younger of the two sons of Ernst I, at the Chapel Royal, St James's Palace in London on 10 February 1840. She longed to see Albert's home country but the first five years of her marriage were tied up having four babies. 1845 was a gap year from her constant pregnancies and she was free to come. It was an emotional moment when she made her official entry into Coburg, driving in an open carriage across the Schloss-platz and into Ehrenburg where the whole family were assembled in full dress to greet her.

I cannot say how much affected I felt in entering this dear old Place & with difficulty I resisted crying: the beautifully ornamented town, all with wreaths & flowers – the numbers of good & affectionate people – the many recollections connected with this place, all was so affecting[4].

The marriage of Victoria and Albert is one of the most famous relationships in history and their story is constantly being retold in different ways. I was pleased to find a poster outside Ehrenburg advertising a musical playing in the ballroom called *Albert & Victoria* (that way round, rather than Victoria & Albert as we always say in Britain). The frosty attendant in the shop was at pains to stress that we would not see the ballroom on the guided tour because it was set up as a theatre, but our guide was more jovial and took us in there anyway. I stood on the temporary stage and marvelled – because this room, called the Giants Hall (Riesensaal), is unlike anything else I have seen!

The Dukes of Saxe-Coburg and Gotha

The dukes of Saxe-Coburg and Gotha were a branch of the Ernestine line of the ancient house of Wettin which can trace its ancestry back to the tenth century and beyond. In 1485 there was a lasting split when two brothers, Ernest and Albert, divided the house into two lines – the Ernestine and the Albertine. The Ernestine line went through further divisions and reorganisations and from this line were descended several royal families of Germany before World War I, including that of Saxe-Coburg and Gotha.

The combined duchy of Saxe-Coburg and Gotha came into being in 1826, on a reorganisation of Ernestine lands following the death (without a male heir) of the last duke of another Ernestine branch. Prior to this the name of the duchy was Saxe-Coburg-Saalfeld. In the 1826 reshuffle, Duke Ernst III of Saxe-Coburg-Saalfeld ceded his Saalfeld lands to yet another Ernestine branch and obtained Gotha instead. He then became Duke Ernst I of Saxe-Coburg and Gotha. Ernst I now ruled a double duchy with twin residences in Coburg and Gotha and the family name became Saxe-Coburg and Gotha. But when almost ninety years later the monarchy fell, the separate history of the two pulled them in different directions. The citizens of Coburg voted to become part of Bavaria, leaving Gotha as part of another state called Thuringia. This would have profound consequences after World War II when Thuringia (but not Bavaria) fell behind the Iron Curtain.

The Giants Hall dates from the baroque remodelling of Ehrenburg by Duke Albrecht in the 1690s. The room takes its name from twenty-eight muscular stucco (plasterwork) figures that line the walls and (like Atlas holding up the world) support the ceiling cornice on their shoulders. One arm of each giant is raised to help take the weight of the burden, the other is outstretched and holds a candelabra. The height of the hall is low relative to its size and the effect of the ornate stuccoed ceiling and the masterful, struggling figures was quite overpowering. This room hosted many important occasions and has a role in British royal history. Victoria's parents were

23. A drawing of the rear view of Ehrenburg.

married here on 29 May 1818[5], and fifteen-year-old Albert (with his elder brother) was examined here in front of an audience (of family, clergy, and representatives of the people of Coburg) on 11 April 1835, before his confirmation.

I was unprepared for the splendour of Ehrenburg because I came with the idea that Albert was a poor prince. When she announced her engagement, Victoria's choice of husband was not popular with the British public who regarded him as a fortune hunter. A verse in the street ballads complained that

> Prince Albert was a petty prince,
> A petty prince of low degree
> He left the starved country of his birth
> For a good birth in this fine countrie[6]

But walking through the magnificent rooms of their schloss, the idea that the Coburg family were paupers seemed ridiculous! The highlight for me was the Gobelin Room, with eighteenth century French tapestries (bought by Ernst I) on the walls and an astonishing three-dimensional stuccowork ceiling from 1692, with garlands of flowers and oak leaves that hang down naturalistically into the room. A semi-circular bulge in the corner of this room shows where a lift was installed for Victoria (now elderly) when she stayed at the schloss to attend a family wedding in April 1894[7]. Victoria's bedroom is included on the tour (it is the middle window on the second floor of the left hand side wing in illustration 21). The guide opened the door of what resembled a large wardrobe next to the bed and inside was her mahogany-clad private loo – made in England in 1860 and one of the first water closets on the continent.

Directly beneath those of Queen Victoria are the rooms of Albert's mother, Duchess Luise, who disappeared from his life when he was five years old. Her elegant bedroom, hung with draped green silk, was modelled on that of Empress Josephine at Chateau Malmaison outside Paris. The marriage of Ernst I and Luise was unhappy and he used the double standards of his day, about their sexual peccadillos, to force a separation and later on a divorce (for more on this story see Schloss Friedenstein in *Schloss II*). Luise was popular in the duchy and Ehrenburg was the scene of some dramatic events at the end of the marriage when the people of Coburg rose up in protest against her exile[8]. The protestors were hoping for a reconciliation and forced Ernst and Luise to appear together on a balcony at Ehrenburg. But their demonstration was of no avail; Luise was separated from her sons and sent away. She wrote

Parting from my children was the worst thing of all. They have whooping cough and they said 'Mamma is crying because she has to go away while we are ill'[9].

Rosenau

Prince Albert was born in a beguiling small castle at Rödental near Coburg called Schloss Rosenau. He spent summers here as a child with his elder brother and it was always associated in his mind with the carefree days of childhood before he left for England. This was Albert's favourite home and when he brought Victoria on her first visit to Coburg in 1845, they stayed at Rosenau. The schloss would always be special for her too and Victoria wrote in her journal,

If I were not who I am [Queen of England], – this would have been my real home, but I shall always consider it my 2nd one. Albert is so, so happy to be here with me, – it is like a beautiful dream[10].

Albert's grandfather acquired the schloss and his father, Ernst I, renovated it in neo-gothic style after he became the duke in 1806. The work was finished in time to celebrate his marriage to Duchess Luise in 1817 with a medieval pageant in the grounds. Their second child, Albert, was born at Rosenau on 26 August 1819 and christened three weeks later (19 September) in the Marble Hall. This is the

Schloss Rosenau bei Coburg

main reception room with a dazzling confection of white marble pillars and gold filigree decoration.

With the end of the monarchy, Rosenau passed into the ownership of the state and after World War II it was used as an old people's home. When I visited for the first time in 1981, the home had closed and the schloss was empty, sad, and abandoned. Happily, it then underwent a major restoration and opened as a museum. This is a really nice place to visit.

Because her marriage and her life were short (she died at thirty) portraits of Luise are rare but there are two at Ehrenburg. Family portraits are a feature of the schloss and I knew I was in for a treat when there were ten in the first room on the tour. None of the portraits were labelled, which could have been so frustrating except that our jovial guide was happy to name them all. As well as Albert and Victoria, they included Albert's older brother Ernst II (1818-1893) and his wife Alexandrine.

As children, Ernst and Albert were very close and had never been separated before Ernst joined the Saxon army to begin his military training in 1838. But as men the two had a very different attitude to sex. Albert had an abhorrence of sexual immorality and was completely faithful to Victoria, whereas Ernst was a libertine and often unfaithful to his wife. He was initiated young into the fleshpots by their father[11] and was already suffering from a sexually transmitted disease when he accompanied his brother to England in 1839, so Victoria could inspect Albert as a potential bridegroom[12]. A possible reason why Alexandrine had no children is that Ernst infected her and the disease made her sterile. So the Coburg succession fell to Victoria and Albert's sons and proved a poisoned chalice that uprooted two of their grandsons as English schoolboys and forced them to become German. (See chart 4 for the succession to the duchy of Saxe-Coburg and Gotha).

The succession fell first on Victoria and Albert's second son Alfred, duke of Edinburgh (1844-1900). Affie (as he was known) was a naval officer who retired

24. The Palais Edinburgh was bought in 1866 for Queen Victoria's second son Alfred, the designated heir to Coburg.

with the rank of Admiral of the Fleet. His whole heart was in England and the British navy. But his Uncle Ernst's death meant that he had to take up his responsibilities in Coburg where his wife and family were already living in the Palais Edinburgh (on the opposite side of Schloss-platz to Ehrenburg). Awkward questions were raised in Britain about whether a German duke should sit in the House of Lords, and in Germany over on which side a retired British admiral would be in event of war! Affie became more difficult, drank too much, and died a few years later. His only son, who should have been next in line for the duchy, had died the year before him – aged twenty-four.

25. Duke Alfred and his wife Grand Duchess Marie Alexandrovna.

Young Affie (1874-1899) was sent to Germany as a child to be educated as a German prince, and thereafter only saw his parents and four sisters occasionally. Perhaps this made him rootless and was a factor when he went off the rails as a young officer in the Prussian army. His mother's letters to one sister include a string of complaints about how '... he has to leave the regiment almost in disgrace ...'; '... his nasty illness which has attacked the brain ...' (syphilis); and 'A charming son, who pays his low life love affairs with his mother's money!'.

You would be horrified if you saw him and it is a real sad lesson of what a young man can reduce himself [to] by a constant course of vice self indulgence and moral laisser faire[13].

Syphilis was a shameful disease and the circumstances of Young Affie death were hushed up, allowing rumours to circulate. One story is that he was deeply depressed and tried to shoot himself during the celebrations for his parents' twenty-fifth wedding anniversary. This may not be true as, in his memoirs, Prince Andreas, the current head of the house of Saxe-Coburg and Gotha, gives Affie's disease as the cause of death[14]. The young man died away from home in a clinic and Duke Alfred never forgave his wife for hustling their son out of the house when he was mortally ill, because she was ashamed of him.

Affie's death meant that the Saxe-Coburg and Gotha succession passed to another English schoolboy, as we find out at the next schloss.

Veste Coburg

26. In the background, the old fortress castle of the dukes of Coburg, called Veste Coburg, towers above the town.

The old fortress castle of the dukes of Coburg, called Veste Coburg, came into the ancestral house of the dukes of Saxe-Coburg and Gotha in 1353. The Veste towers one hundred and sixty-seven metres above the town and features in many old prints of Coburg (see illustration 26). The climb up from the town is steep but, if you don't fancy the equivalent of around fifty flights of stairs, you can always take the little train that does city tours. Entrance to the Veste is through the Grand Portal, built in baroque style in 1671, and into a courtyard where (to my immense surprise) in front of us was an early twentieth-century building, resembling a mock-tudor English country house. The Fürstenbau (Prince's Wing) was built by the last reigning duke of Saxe-Coburg and Gotha, who was Karl Eduard (1884-1954). He lost his throne, with all the other German princes, at the end of World War I.

Karl Eduard was the second English schoolboy to be affected by the Coburg succession. He was born as Prince Charles Edward of Albany and was the posthumous son of Victoria's and Albert's youngest son, Leopold, duke of Albany. Leopold had the bleeding disease (haemophilia) which blighted Victoria's descendants, and died aged thirty following a fall. When the death of Young Affie in 1899 (see Ehrenburg above) reopened the question of who would succeed to Coburg, the choice fell on Leopold's only son (see chart 4)[15]. The following year Duke Alfred died and sixteen-year-old Charlie (as he was called) was taken away from Eton to be educated in Germany under the supervision of his cousin, Kaiser Wilhelm II. His name was germanised to Karl Eduard. Charlie would turn out be a dark spot in the family history.

As a British prince succeeding to a German throne, poor Charlie was caught in a cleft stick. He was on the opposite side to his mother and sister in World War I and was stripped of his British rank and titles. But in Germany his English origins made him suspect and there were loud objections to the wealth of the Coburg family going to a British prince. Perhaps he over-compensated by trying to become 'more German than the Germans'? In the 1930s Karl Eduard joined the Nazi party and became a firm follower of Hitler. He undertook diplomatic missions for the Nazis and was referred to in the international press as *Hitler's Duke*[16]. Like many other Germans he must have harked back to what he saw as better times before the war and may have hoped that Hitler would restore the princes to their thrones.

Karl Eduard was the president of the German Red Cross during World War II, and by this time it had ceased to be a humanitarian organisation and was implementing Hitler's euthanasia policies. In his later interrogation, Karl Eduard categorically denied any knowledge of the Nazi atrocities and it is hard to assess the truth of this. On the one hand there seems no direct evidence that he was involved; but on the other, as president of the Red Cross surely he must have known? It is of great credit that the present head of house, Prince Andreas of Saxe-Coburg-Gotha, talked about his grandfather's Nazi sympathies in his recent memoirs[17] and has also opened the house archives to researchers on the topic[18].

27. Duke Karl Eduard – the last reigning duke of Saxe-Coburg and Gotha.

Almost as soon as he reached his twenty-first birthday and took over the reins as duke, Karl Eduard began a radical building programme at Veste Coburg, working with the famous castle enthusiast and architect Bodo Ebhardt (he lived in his own castle on the Rhine – see Schloss Marksburg in *Schloss*). They undid the nineteenth century restoration work of Dukes Ernst I and Ernst II, and put up several new buildings on the site of old ones. These included the building that surprised me –

the Fürstenbau or Prince's Wing, a grand new residence for the duke and his family built between 1906 and 1920 in historicist style (imitation of the architecture of the past) but with all the latest modern conveniences. Other new buildings were the Luther Chapel (1909-1913), the Duchess's Wing (1917-1921), and the Karl Eduard Wing (completed 1924). The building programme continued even after Karl Eduard was forced to abdicate in November 1918. Veste Coburg was taken over by the new Free State but the settlement negotiated by the ex-duke included (as well as monetary compensation) the right to live in the Prince's Wing.

28. The Fürstenbau (Prince's Wing) was built in the early twentieth century.

Karl Eduard's buildings all now form part of an important museum at Veste Coburg formed around the vast ducal art collections (*Kunst Sammlungen der Veste Coburg*). The Coburgs were passionate collectors and the museum includes (just as a few examples) the Venetian glass collection of Duke Alfred (1844-1900); a coin collection purchased by Alfred's father Albert Prince Consort (1819-1861) and the medals and decorations of his cousin, Tsar Ferdinand of Bulgaria (1861-1948). It also houses a huge collection of prints amassed by Albert's grandfather Duke Franz Friedrich Anton (1750-1806); and the Turkish war booty of Duke Franz's uncle Prince Friedrich Josias (1737-1815) who was a general in the Austrian army. The two wedding coaches of Duke Johann Casimir (1564-1633) are the oldest surviving ceremonial carriages in Europe. Johann Casimir divorced his first wife Anna for adultery and shut her away in a nunnery. When he married again he had a medal minted to further humiliate his ex-wife. The front side shows a couple kissing with the caption 'A lover's kiss is such sweet fun', but the reverse depicts a nun with the rhyme 'Who will kiss a wretched nun?'[19].

29. The Grand Portal, built in 1671.

We visited the museum in the Prince's Wing to see the rooms fitted out by Bodo Ebhardt for Karl Eduard's grand residence. These are a strange mixture and show how the architect imitated the styles of the past whilst at the same time incorporating the latest technology. The living room of the guest apartment on the first floor is planked-out in the style of 1500, but the bathroom next door has white porcelain and tiled walls from the twentieth century. In the Duke and Duchess's apartment on the second floor, the Cranach Room was used by Karl Eduard as a sitting room. The paintings by Lucas Cranach the Elder and the sixteenth-century stained glass in the window are original; but the neo-renaissance panelling was installed by Bodo and hides the radiators for the central heating!

There is a huge amount to see at Veste Coburg and with translation everywhere this museum is readily accessible to an English-speaking visitor. My only complaint is that when we looked for the advertised cafeteria it was hard to find, and when we got there it turned out to be a vending machine! Come on Veste Coburg – you can do better than that for your tired visitors!

Callenberg

30. Callenberg was a wedding present to Duke Ernst II and
Duchess Alexandrine of Saxe-Coburg and Gotha.

In May 1842, Prince Ernst of Saxe-Coburg and Gotha (1818-1893),
the future Duke Ernst II, married Alexandrine of Baden. His father
(Duke Ernst I) gave the young couple Callenberg as a wedding present.
The schloss had been acquired by Ernst I in the reorganisation of
family lands and properties in 1826. Like father like son, Ernst II was
not a good husband. He was frequently unfaithful to his wife and when
it became clear she would have no children, took little further interest
in her. But, despite this neglect, Alexandrine remained a devoted wife.
They were married for fifty-one years and their *Golden Wedding Crown*
is on display at Callenberg – a delicate circlet with a tracery of golden
leaves and flower buds tied at the back with a golden bow. Alongside
the crown is a photo of husband and wife in their golden wedding year
in which Alexandrine still gazes adoringly at an unprepossessing Ernst.
His great-niece (who became Queen of Romania) described the elderly
Ernst II as follows –

...an old beau, squeezed into a frock coat too tight for his bulk and uncomfortably pinched in at the waist...[20]

But what a spectacular wedding present! Callenberg has a stunning hilltop location, surrounded by trees, just five kilometres outside the town of Coburg. The day was misty and it rained throughout our visit, but nothing could spoil the charm of the schloss or the views out over the countryside, described by Queen Victoria on a visit to Coburg in 1860 as 'glorious' when she lunched here with her sister-in-law, Duchess Alexandrine, while Albert went out shooting [21]. Victoria was sketching the view of Coburg from the terrace at Callenberg just before Albert had a bad carriage accident that left him shocked and with a premonition he would never see his home country again after this trip[22]. Victoria's sketch is still preserved in the royal archives at Windsor Castle near London (with a note in her own handwriting that it was done just before the accident).

Callenberg is on two levels, with an Oberschloss (upper castle) restored by Ernst I in 1831, and an Unterschloss (lower castle) restored by his son, Ernst II, in 1856-1857. I particularly liked the upper castle where the main reception room (called the Roter Salon or Red Room) opens directly onto a rose garden. This pretty garden has geometric beds of roses, arranged around a central fountain and set off by low box hedging and yew topiary. I did a double-take when I noticed that the four statues (one at each corner of the fountain) are the figures of naked tennis players! The flower beds are planted with roses named after royal ladies in countries where the throne descends from the Saxe-Coburg and Gotha family. *La Reine Victoria* is an old shrub rose from 1872, and has clusters of scented pink-lilac blooms. It is named (of course) after Queen Victoria whose mother was a Coburg (she was the sister of Ernst I). Even older is *Rose Princess Louise*, a fragrant light-pink rambling rose originally cultivated in France in 1829. Louise was the French princess who married Leopold I (the youngest brother of Ernst I) as his second wife, after he became the first king of Belgium in 1831. In 1905, Duke Karl Eduard married a German princess and *Herzogin Victoria Adelheid of Coburg-Gotha* is an icy-pink hybrid tea rose, named that year in her honour. Karl Eduard and Victoria Adelheid used Callenberg as a summer home and their daughter Sibylla celebrated her engagement, to the heir to the Swedish throne, in the Roter Salon in 1932. *Crown Princess Victoria of Sweden* is named after Sibylla's granddaughter, who is the current Swedish heir. This vibrant red rose, introduced in 1986, has no thorns.

31. The rose garden at Callenberg is planted with roses named after royal ladies in the Coburg family.

Callenberg remained the property of Karl Eduard after 1918 and is now owned by the Saxe-Coburg and Gotha Family Foundation. The Ducal Art Exhibition in the schloss uses a remarkable collection of portraits to tell the fascinating story of this family's rise in prominence during the nineteenth century. Hung together as a family group, are the portraits of Duke Franz Friedrich Anton (1750-1806), his second wife Duchess Augusta (1757-1831), and the seven of their children who survived infancy – three brothers and four sisters (including Albert's father and Victoria's mother). The family's fortunes were founded on a successful marriage strategy and in a period of six short years in the 1830s, three thrones came out of the marriages of this generation of children. And more thrones would follow in the future. (Chart 5 in appendix C is a list of the children of Franz Friedrich Anton and Augusta showing the thrones descended from them.)

It all began in 1795 when Tsarina Catherine the Great of Russia invited Duchess Augusta to bring her three teenaged daughters to St Petersburg on inspection as a bride. Catherine was looking for a wife for her sixteen-year-old grandson, Grand Duke Constantine (the younger brother of the future Tsar Alexander I). The often-repeated story (which is probably not true) is that when Constantine was pressed to make a choice between the three he did so arbitrarily, based on how they alighted from a carriage. The eldest, Sophia, got tangled up in her train and fell out; the second, Antoinette, crawled out on all-fours to avoid the same fate; and only the youngest, fourteen-year-old Juliane, showed any grace[23]. Whatever the truth of the story, it does show how little choice Constantine was given. Little Juliane was given even less: she was expected to say 'Yes' and then left behind in Russia to convert to the Orthodox faith and prepare for her wedding. Constantine was out-of-control and proved to be a nasty husband, '... who was subject to sudden and violent rages ... and committed deeds of cruelty.[24]' Juliane earned the sympathy of her brother-in-law Alexander and after he became tsar in 1801, he gave her permission to go home to Coburg[25].

But Juliane's connection to the important Russian court brought benefits for her family. Her youngest brother Leopold became an officer in the Russian army and a favourite with the tsar. In 1814 he came to London as part of Alexander's suite, where he met Princess Charlotte of Great Britain and paid court to her. Charlotte was the only child of the prince regent (later George IV) and the next heir to the British throne after her father. Leopold wanted to marry Charlotte out of ambition and Charlotte's emotions were in turmoil. She had just jilted the fiancé selected by her father and fancied she was in love with another prince who did not meet with her father's approval.

It did not seem likely that he would think Leopold – the younger son of a minor German duke – any more suitable. But amazingly Charlotte and Leopold fell in love, the tsar was in favour, the prince regent gave his consent, and they were married in May 1816. As husband of the heiress to the British throne, Leopold had made his fortune.

But their happiness was short-lived. Charlotte died in November 1817 giving birth to their stillborn son. Leopold was devastated by grief, but as time passed his ambition re-emerged. His marriage had made him a player on the European scene and if he could not be king consort of Great Britain; he would try for a throne of his own. In 1831 Leopold became the first king of Belgium, a new country just made independent of the Netherlands. The present king of Belgium, King Philippe, is Leopold's great-great-great-grandson[26].

Leopold was a driving force behind the marriage of his sister Victoire, which would bring another Coburg throne. In 1818 Victoire married, as her second husband, Edward Duke of Kent. Her mother, Duchess Augusta, commented that she hoped this marriage (to a man Victoire had barely met) would bring her child the happiness lacking in the first[27]. Kent was the fourth son of King George III of Great Britain and the marriage was important as, following Charlotte's death, any children would be in the running for the British crown. Their only child was a daughter

32. Prince Leopold of Saxe-Coburg became the first king of Belgium in 1831.

born on 24 May 1819 and Kent died when the baby was eight-months-old. She succeeded to the British throne, as Queen Victoria, in 1837.

In 1840 Victoria married her Coburg first cousin Albert, the son of her mother's eldest brother Ernst I (see chart 4). They founded the Saxe-Coburg and Gotha dynasty of Great Britain and Queen Elizabeth II is their great-great-granddaughter. As a new bride Victoria said she did not want to have a large family, but she became the matriarch of a huge clan with forty grandchildren and twenty-seven great-grandchildren before she died. There are portraits of Victoria and Albert's nine children hung together in one room at Callenberg. They and their children married into Europe's royal families and several more thrones would descend from this group of siblings[28]. This Coburg spider's web led to tragic consequences in World War I with family members on both sides of conflict; King George V of Great Britain was a first cousin of Kaiser Wilhelm II of Germany.

Portugal was the third throne that came to the family when Ferdinand (a Coburg cousin of Victoria and Albert) married the seventeen-year-old Queen Maria II da Gloria in 1836. Their descendants reigned in Portugal until the monarchy was abolished in 1910 and the last king of Portugal, Manoel, was their great-grandson[29].

I was impressed with how the exhibition at Callenberg told the story of the Coburg thrones, using large-scale family trees, laminated handouts (all translated into English), and their large collection of portraits. The story is brought up to date with portraits and biographies of the current head of house, Prince Andreas, and his family. Andreas (born in 1943) is the grandson of Duke Karl Eduard. His parents' war-time marriage did not last and, after his mother remarried an American officer, Andreas was brought up in the USA. When he returned to Germany to do his military service in the early 1960s, he had to relearn how to speak German. This distance has enabled him to take an independent view of his heritage and he entitled his published memoirs 'I did it my way ...'[30].

Ketschendorf

Schloss Ketschendorf, on the outskirts of Coburg, has a chequered history. It was built at the beginning of the nineteenth century by the formidable Duchess Augusta of Saxe-Coburg-Saalfeld (1757-1831), who was the guiding hand behind the Coburg marriage strategy and the grandmother of both Queen Victoria and Prince Albert (see charts 4 and 5). Duchess Augusta used it as a summer residence after she was widowed in 1806 and there are many references in her diary to the happy times she spent at Ketschendorf. In the diary entry for her first day staying at the schloss in 1817, she wrote

> I have not been able to withstand any longer the call of the nightingales and spring, and remained here for the night. When I move into town in the Autumn, the time spent until I return again here to my peaceful little home seems like an eternity[31].

After Augusta's death in 1831, Ketschendorf became the property of her daughter-in-law Duchess Marie (the second wife of Ernst I) and after her death in 1860, it passed to Ernst II (Albert's elder brother). In 1866 he sold it to his mistress – a famous French soprano who had starred at the Paris opera under the stage name of Rosine Stoltz. She put up a new building on the site and demolished the original building of Duchess Augusta in 1869. But almost as soon as her new schloss was finished, Rosine sold it and moved back to Paris.

In World War II Ketschendorf was expropriated from a Jewish family by the Nazis and the schloss and surrounding park were bought by the town of Coburg. The mother of a friend of mine, who lived in Coburg at this time as a child, remembers the excitement of the contents being auctioned off. The property was returned to its pre-war owners after the war in reparation, but sold back almost immediately to the town of Coburg. In the 1950s the schloss became a youth hostel and, some years later, a new building was added in the grounds, right next to Rosine's schloss, to provide extra accommodation. The grounds of Ketschendorf were opened as a public park.

The youth hostel closed in 2010 and in 2013 the empty schloss was acquired by a company head-quartered in Coburg called Kaeser Kompressoren. Kaeser are now carrying out a major renovation and when we visited (in 2016) the building was shrouded in scaffolding. When completed, the schloss will be used as a company training centre with meeting rooms available to the public as well as for company use. The original décor of the ground floor is still in place and will be restored, although the top floors were long since altered by previous owners. The Youth Hostel building has already been by converted by Kaeser into accommodation for their apprentices. It is very good news that this historic building will get a new lease of life with sympathetic owners and I can't wait to visit when it's finished!

Ketschendorf is familiar to many Germans as the location for a trilogy of fantasy films about a time-travelling teenager called Ruby Red (2013),

Sapphire Blue (2014,) and Emerald Green (2016), based on the novel by Kerstin Gier. The photo to the left is of the inside of the schloss during filming. Schloss Ehrenburg (see above) also features in the series – as a London secondary school.

4

REGENSBURG
AND THE PRINCES OF
THURN UND TAXIS

The city of Regensburg is the capital of the Upper Palatinate region of the federal state of Bavaria (see the map in appendix A). It may be better known to readers by its Latin name of Ratisbon which is often used in the history books. In 1245 Regensburg became independent from the duke of Bavaria and was granted self-governing status as an imperial free city of the Holy Roman Empire. From that time Regensburg was often the Holy Roman emperor's location of choice to convene an imperial diet (the official assembly or parliament of the different territories in the Empire). From 1594 every imperial diet was held in Regensburg.

The diet called by the emperor at Regensburg in 1663 was never officially adjourned and continued in session in the city right up until the end of the Empire in 1806. Known as the *Perpetual Diet*, it has been called the forerunner of the European parliament. After a while the ruling princes of the different territories no longer attended in person but sent ambassadors instead, and the emperor was represented in

Regensburg by a prince appointed as his principal commissioner. This prince had to be of high rank and also very rich indeed, since the costs of representing the emperor and hosting court life always far exceeded the salary.

St Emmeram

The illustration on the next page commemorates the arrival in Regensburg in 1748, as principal commissioner for Emperor Karl VII, of Prince Alexander Ferdinand of Thurn und Taxis. From that time on until the end of the Empire, the position was held continuously by three successive princes of this fabulously wealthy family. The throne, on which these commissioners sat to host the proceedings, and receive foreign envoys on behalf of the emperor, is still preserved in their schloss in Regensburg, called St Emmeram. (Please see chart 6 for a family tree of the princes of Thurn und Taxis in Regensburg.)

St Emmeram (sometimes known as Schloss Thurn und Taxis) came into the ownership of the family in 1812. For a thousand years before this it was a Benedictine monastery (founded at the burial place of Saint Emmeram) and an important centre of art and learning. The monastery was dissolved in 1810 and the buildings then given to Prince Karl Alexander of Thurn und Taxis as compensation for the nationalisation of the family's postal business in Bavaria (see text box on page 71). Building work started straightaway, and went on throughout the nineteenth century, to convert the monks' cells and administrative buildings into a grand princely palace with lavishly decorated interiors. The schloss has a vast footprint which incorporates the old monastery basilica of St Emmeram (now a parish church) and the old cloisters (part of the museum tour). With five hundred rooms, fourteen staircases, and over fourteen thousand square metres of parquet, St Emmeram is even bigger than Buckingham Palace in London!

The first thing that strikes you on a visit is the big personality of Princess Gloria of Thurn und Taxis. Large photos of the princess with

33. Double portrait of Prince Alexander Ferdinand (1704-1773) and
Prince Albert (1867-1952), commemorating 150 years of
Thurn und Taxis in Regensburg.

various celebrities (Michael Jackson, Liza Minelli) adorn the ticket
office and shop, her portrait is on the cover of the guidebook, and the
café is called Café Gloria. The princess is a collector of avant-garde
art and almost the first thing we saw on the guided tour was a huge
and grubby-looking fried egg hanging down the stairwell of the Marble
Staircase! This was a present from Princess Gloria to her late husband,
Prince Johannes of Thurn und Taxis (1926-1990), on his sixtieth
birthday. Later on the tour we saw *Living Portraits* of the princess and
her three children; these are photographs projected on a large video
screen, with eyes that blink. I didn't like the art, but I do admire how
Princess Gloria rescued the family fortunes and put St Emmeram on a
commercial footing after her husband's death.

The life story of Princess Gloria is a modern-day fairy tale. She
was a nineteen-year-old student at acting school when she chanced to
meet the fifty-three-year-old prince of Thurn und Taxis. After a short

romance they married in the basilica at St Emmeram on 31 May 1980. Johannes was immensely wealthy and for the next few years the couple lived a jet-set life, travelling between homes around the world. Gloria has described how she shopped in couture houses, stayed at the Ritz in Paris, and was photographed for *Vogue*[1]. Her spikey taste in clothes and love of modern art earned her the nicknames of *Princess Punk* and *Princess TNT* in the gossip columns[2]. But when her husband became ill

34. The south wing of St Emmeram in an old picture.

and died from heart disease, Gloria discovered their finances were in a mess, their debts huge, and the Thurn und Taxis commercial ventures losing millions. With no experience of business or finance, thirty-year-old Gloria had to step in and take over as head of house on behalf of her seven-year-old son, Albert. And like a fairy-tale, the story has a happy ending. She rose to the challenge with tough decisions, cost-cutting, and retrenchment, and proved to have considerable commercial acumen. St Emmeram is a great place to visit today, with tours leaving every half hour and an excellent English guidebook. Gloria did not have an acting career but her flamboyant personality has meant she has never been out of the limelight. Her lavishly illustrated book about the family and their schloss includes photos of her own extraordinary private apartments (not shown on the tour) decorated with modern works of art[3].

The Thurn und Taxis family and the postal service

The history of the Thurn und Taxis began very differently from that of the other German noble families. In 1490 an Italian ancestor called Francesco Tasso (1459-1517) founded the fortunes of the house when he set up the first ever postal service. The route ran from Innsbruck in Austria to Brussels and, by dint of the innovative idea of using relays of horses and riders, took only a week to get there. It was a break-through in communications across the Holy Roman Empire and a grateful Emperor Maximillian I ennobled the inventor of the post as Franz von Taxis. Sometime later (I don't know when) their name changed to Thurn und Taxis.

For generations the Thurn und Taxis ran the postal service for the Holy Roman Empire and in 1615 the title of imperial postmaster general was made hereditary in the family. They became fabulously rich from the profits and rose steadily in rank – to baron (freiherr) in 1608, count (graf) in 1624, and finally to prince (fürst) in 1695. In its eighteenth century heyday the Thurn und Taxis imperial postal service ran from the Baltic in the north of the Empire to the Alps in the south, and from the Netherlands in the west to Austria and the Adriatic in the east.

But the French Revolution ushered in a period of great difficulty for the family business. The wars with France disrupted the postal service so that for the first time ever the accounts showed a loss[4]. Worse followed when the Empire was dissolved in 1806, and the right to run the imperial service became null and void. Some German states nationalised their postal service and not all of them paid compensation to the Thurn und Taxis. At the end of 1810, there were forty-three different operators across Germany. Prince Karl Alexander wrote to his wife that the good times were over and she must economise[5].

It was not until the Congress of Vienna in 1815, at the end of the Napoleonic Wars, that the Thurn und Taxis family were given back the right to run the post in some parts of the new German Confederation. These new rights lasted until 1867, when Bismarck nationalised the postal service across the German states.

35. The tour begins by the Electors' Fountain in the Inner Courtyard.

The guided tour at St Emmeram takes the visitor through a suite of rooms called the Princely State Rooms. The words that come to mind to describe them are – opulent, luxuriant, and extravagant! Before the family came to Regensburg their main residence was a schloss in Frankfurt (destroyed by bombing in World War II) and whole rooms were stripped out from there and moved to St Emmeram. The light and glittering White Hall (or ballroom), with charming rococo décor and huge gold and crystal chandeliers, was originally created for the Frankfurt schloss in 1730 and reinstalled at St Emmeram in 1890. This is where Prince Johannes and Princess Gloria had their wedding reception. The gorgeous and glowing Yellow Salon, also in playful rococo style, is another room relocated from Frankfurt. The dimensions were not the same and you can see where the mirrors were cut to fit the reduced ceiling height.

One of the things I liked about St Emmeram was the focus given to the women in the Thurn und Taxis family and how, on the guided tour, their stories are interwoven with the history of the rooms. Princess Gloria was not the first to have to manage the family business through a crisis. Gräfin Alexandrine has been called one of the greatest women in the history of the house for her achievement in managing the post through the awful conditions of the Thirty Years War in Germany (1618-1648)[6]. When her husband died in 1628 Alexandrine had to take over as postmaster on behalf of her eight-year-old son and she kept it going through war, plunder, and destitution until he took over in 1646.

During the turmoil caused in Germany by the Napoleonic Wars (1802-1815), Princess Therese went to Paris to try her hand at persuading Napoleon to allow the Thurn und Taxis to run the post in the new empire he was creating. She offered to move the family to Paris if he would agree. Therese was the wife of Karl Alexander (1770-1827), the first Thurn und Taxis to reside at St Emmeram. She had no success with Napoleon, and probably it didn't help that the French censors were reading her letters to the enemy in the form of her sister Queen Luise of Prussia (the sisters were born princesses of Mecklenburg-Strelitz and were the nieces of Queen Charlotte of Great Britain). But after Napoleon's final defeat, Therese's generous hospitality and skilful politicking at the Congress of Vienna were important in securing the family a new grant of rights. Therese's elegant bedroom at St Emmeram, called the Green Salon, was one of my favourite rooms. It was created in 1812 in the fashionable French empire style and has an amazing golden bed with four golden swans as legs. Their wings are outspread and their long necks droop gracefully to touch the floor.

But the room that had the biggest impact on me was the staggering Silver Salon, commissioned by Princess Helene in 1873. Everything you can imagine in this room is made or gilded with silver – panelling, plasterwork, furniture, and stunning chandelier. And due to a technical innovation the silver has never lost its original shine; it is in fact a copper alloy with a percentage of silver, which will never tarnish. I was delighted to find Princess Helene at St Emmeram, because she had a supporting role in a very famous royal story and I had often wondered what happened to her afterwards. Helene (called *Néné* in her family) was the elder sister of Empress Elisabeth of Austria (called *Sisi*); and it was *Néné* (not *Sisi*) who was supposed to marry their cousin Emperor

36. The beautiful Empress Elisabeth of Austria often visited St Emmeram to see her sister, Princess Helene.

Franz Joseph. The intended marriage was cooked up by their mothers, who were sisters, but when *Néné* was taken to meet Franz Joseph so that he could propose, he preferred her fifteen-year-old younger sister instead. Franz Joseph and *Sisi* were married on 24 April 1854, and rejected *Néné* was back on the shelf.

Four years later, on 24 August 1858, Helene married Prince Maximilian Anton of Thurn und Taxis (1831-1867). The wedding was at her family summer home of Schloss Possenhofen on Lake Starnberg (see Casino, Roseninsel in chapter 6), in a chapel built for the occasion by her father, Duke Maximilian in Bavaria. The couple were in love but they had to break through some barriers to get married. Just as the Hapsburgs of Austria had earlier tried to turn up their noses at Sisi (on the grounds that Duke Maximilian only came from a junior branch of the Wittelsbach family), now the Wittelsbacher did not consider the Thurn und Taxis family to be good enough for *Néné*. King Maximilian II of Bavaria refused his consent and only gave way when Emperor Franz Joseph intervened, at the urging of his wife (*Sisi*). (Please see chart 13 for the marriages of *Néné* and *Sisi*.)

Helene was the acting head of house Thurn und Taxis on behalf of her minor son on two separate occasions (see chart 6). The first was between 1871 and 1883 when her eldest son, Maximilian Maria, succeeded his grandfather as a nine-year-old (Helene's husband had died before his father). Maximilian Maria came of age in 1883 but died of a heart complaint only two years later. So Helene had to step in again until her second son, Albert, reached his twenty-first birthday on 8 May 1888. He bought Schloss Garatshausen on Lake Starnberg (now a nursing home) for his mother to retire near her childhood home of Possenhofen. But Helene didn't have long to live and came back to St Emmeram to die. The last of the Princely State Rooms on the guided tour is the House Chapel, with a wonderful ceiling covered with little golden angel heads and wings. This was Helene's bedroom and she died here, with Sisi at her side, on 16 May 1890. Her son, Albert I, turned it into a chapel dedicated to her memory.

At the end of our visit we walked around the medieval cloisters of the old Benedictine monastery. The carved stonework of the columns and the ribbed gothic arches were a quiet contrast to the ornate and lavish decoration of the Princely State Rooms. In the south cloister, mounted high up on the capstones at the top point of the arches are portraits of five of the fourteenth century abbots. They wanted to be up here for posterity – as close as possible to God.

Burgruine Donastauf

The small town of Donaustauf (ten kilometres east of Regensburg) has a marvellous location on the bank of the Danube in the foothills of the Bavarian forest. As we drove towards it, two historic landmarks were in our sights, hanging on the dark wooded hillside above the town – Burgruine Donastauf and the Walhalla monument. These turned out to be delightful places to visit, but first we bumped into a relic of another schloss in Donastauf – an oddity called the Chinese Tower.

Donastauf was part of the compensation given to Prince Karl Alexander of Thurn und Taxis by the king of Bavaria in 1812, along with St Emmeram (see above). Schloss Donastauf became a favourite summer residence for the Thurn und Taxis family and in 1842 Prince Maximilian Karl (the son of Karl Alexander – see chart 6) erected a pavilion in Chinese style in the garden. The schloss burned down in a catastrophic fire in 1888 which destroyed nearly two-thirds of the town, and has never been rebuilt, but the Chinese Tower in the garden survived. In 1902 the Thurn und Taxis moved it to their new summer residence (Schloss Prüfening on the outskirts of Regensburg) and there it stayed for a hundred years until, in 1999, it was brought back to a new site in Donastauf and restored.

The Chinese Tower is an exotic little building in pagoda style, set in a

 small garden and surrounded by a fence. Its new location is close to the river bank in the centre of town and next to a car park, so that we stumbled on it when parking our car. It is only open to visitors on Sunday afternoons in summer, but not to worry as there is a very good view of the Chinese Tower at any time from just standing on the pavement, outside the fence.

37. The Chinese Tower is all that remains of the Thurn und Taxis summer residence.

Burgruine Donaustauf has a much longer history. This schloss was built in the first half of the tenth century to defend Regensburg against invasions from Hungary. The name Burgruine Donaustauf means ruins of a fortress on a rocky crag above the river Danube (Donau in German) and the schloss looms above the town with a commanding view of the river valley. During the middle ages the fortress saw military action many times and was fiercely contested between three independent territories of the Holy Roman Empire that co-joined in this locality – the Duchy of Bavaria, the Imperial Free City of Regensburg, and the Bishopric of Regensburg.

Donaustauf was destroyed as a fortress during the Thirty Years War (1618-1648). This was a devastating conflict that ravaged the German countryside, bringing famine and plague and killing around a third of the population (historians can only estimate). It was initially a religious conflict between the Protestant and Catholic states in the Holy Roman Empire but later developed into a wider European conflict. Sweden intervened on the side of the Protestant states and in 1630 a Swedish army invaded Germany from the north. In the next few years they reached as far south as Bavaria and menaced or conquered several schlösser. The Swedes besieged and took Donastauf in 1634, then plundered and set it on fire. It was patched up but never properly restored and has been in ruins ever since. Burgruine Donaustauf was part of the compensation package given to the Thurn und Taxis in 1812 and has been owned by the town since 1989.

38. The breath-taking view of the Danube from Burgruine Donastauf.

Although the Burgruine was clearly visible as we drove towards the town, it proved surprisingly difficult to find and there were no signs to help the visitor. Even when we got there we were not sure we were in the right place, until we found an unmanned visitor station with a helpful map of the grounds. Then up we climbed, following a rough winding path, through broken arches and past tumble-down walls of all sorts of different stones and bricks. The ruins have been maintained and made safe, but nature has taken over here and information boards along the path point out the local flora and fauna. There is something romantic about old ruined castles, which is why they were so often painted by Victorian artists. The sun was shining, bees and butterflies crowded the wild flowers, and we wandered happily about. And when we reached the highest point, the views were breath-taking. Below us lay the roofs of Donastauf town and the spire of St Michael's church, with the Danube flowing in a broad curve along the wide valley bottom. And off to the side, peeping out of the trees, was a most impressive but incongruous sight – a Greek temple in the German countryside! This is the Walhalla monument and we just had to visit.

39. King Ludwig I of Bavaria built the Walhalla as a source of German national pride.

The name Walhalla comes from Scandinavian mythology and means the place where the gods greet the souls of dead heroes. King Ludwig I of Bavaria built the Walhalla monument as the German Hall of Fame and it was inaugurated in 1842 with the busts (small statues of the head and shoulders) of ninety-six famous and worthy Germans. Ludwig was born in 1786, just before the French Revolution, and his childhood and youth were overshadowed by French armies marching across the Rhine and through Bavaria. After the break-up of the Holy Roman Empire and the humiliation of the Napoleonic Wars (when much of Germany was under the domination of Napoleon) the king wanted to give Germans back a sense of shared identity and national pride. The site (on Thurn und Taxis land) was chosen very carefully for symbolic reasons; it overlooks the Danube (one of the most important German rivers) and is close to Regensburg (home of the parliament of the Holy Roman Empire).

40. The Walhalla (German Hall of Fame) seen from the other side of the Danube.

Visitors can walk to the Walhalla up the long flights of three hundred and fifty-eight steps or, as we did, drive partway up and have a shorter climb. I was taken aback by the scary signs, warning 'Danger of accident' and 'Stay within the white lines', so that I formed the impression of a decrepit and crumbling building. But as we went up, I could see that the Walhalla is in good condition so I can only think the signs must refer to the steep drops from the steps and terraces. There are no handrails and if anyone fell or jumped from here, they would be seriously injured. It is well worth the effort of the climb because the panorama from the top is just incredible – this must be one of the best views in the world – and the inside is just sublime! The inside of the Walhalla is one huge hall, clad in pink and grey marble and lit by skylights in the roof. All around the walls are the white marble busts of the so-called 'Walhalla comrades'; the ninety-six German heroes originally chosen by Ludwig I and others added later. The first section I looked at included the Holy Roman Emperor Friedrich I Barbarossa, Empress Catherine the Great of Russia (she was German – see Jever in *Schloss II*), the painter Albrecht Dürer, composer Wolfgang Amadeus Mozart, poet Friedrich Schiller, and philosopher Immanuel Kant. At the far end of the hall, across a beautiful mosaic floor studded with gold stars set into white marble squares, is a full-size statue of a seated King Ludwig I wearing Roman robes and a laurel crown. Pictures of the hall do not do justice to the real thing; in my postcards it appears rather ponderous and heavy, whereas in reality this room was full of energy, power, and light. Walking around and reading all the names was a humbling experience – here are the achievements of man but also their craving for power. Alongside Martin Luther and Nicolaus Copernicus were Otto von Bismarck and Kaiser Wilhelm I!

Among the new additions was a face and name I did not know – a young woman called Sophie Scholl. When I asked the museum attendant, sitting in a small glass booth just inside the hall, she told me that Sophie was a University student who founded an anti-Nazi resistance group called *The White Rose* during World War II and was executed aged twenty-one.

5

BAVARIA AND THE WITTELSBACH DUKES AND ELECTORS

From 1180, when Otto of Wittelsbach was created duke of Bavaria, the history of Bavaria is intertwined with the house of Wittelsbach. This ancient royal dynasty survived the twists of fate and time and ruled the region of Bavaria for seven hundred and thirty-eight years. Over the generations, the Wittelsbacher divided and reunited their lands, died out and created new branches of the family, were deposed and reinstated; and finally lost their throne when the German monarchy was overthrown in 1918, at the end of World War I. But even today, when Germany has been a republic for a hundred years, the family are still very popular in Bavaria.

This chapter (and the next) visit schlösser in the region of Bavaria (administrative areas of Upper Bavaria and Lower Bavaria); the heartlands of the Wittelsbacher. The history of the house is long and complicated, but I have tried to highlight parts of their story in relation to these schlösser. This chapter looks at the history of the house in the centuries before Bavaria became a kingdom. We will find a Wittelsbach duke whose celebrity wedding has become the stuff of legend; another who has been called the Bavarian Henry VIII; and the elector of Bavaria who aimed so high that he coveted the Hapsburg thrones of Austria and Spain.

Trausnitz

Trausnitz is the oldest surviving schloss built by the Wittelsbach dynasty in Bavaria. In 1204 Duke Ludwig I (the son of Otto of Wittelsbach) began building a new castle at a place called Landshut (which means stronghold of the countryside). The eight-hundred-year history of his schloss is full of highs and lows, and the nadir came at four am on 21 October 1961 after a cleaning lady forgot to turn off the immersion heater! A fire started and the interior of an important wing called the Fürstenbau (Princes' Building) was reduced to rubble. There are photographs on the guided tour showing the terrible extent of the damage. The building was restored, but much of the historic décor could not be reinstated and for fifty years from 1966 the rooms were

41. Burg Trausnitz is the oldest surviving Wittelsbach schloss in Bavaria.

used to house the state archives. So a visit to Trausnitz is rather a case of what was destroyed and what survived, what has been restored and what has not.

The house of Wittelsbach and the Treaty of Pavia

The long history of the house of Wittelsbach in Bavaria began on 16 September 1180, when Holy Roman Emperor Friedrich I Barbarossa invested Otto of Wittelsbach as duke of Bavaria as a reward for services as his chief military commander and bodyguard. In the next generation another territory (outside Bavaria) called the Palatinate was added to the family possessions when Duke Ludwig I of Bavaria (Otto's son) was also enfeoffed in 1214 as Graf Palatine of the Rhine (the title of the ruler of the Palatinate).

As with the other ancient houses, there were divisions and reorganisations of lands as generations of Wittelsbacher extended their territory or divided the inheritance between brothers. Under the Treaty of Pavia of 1329 there was a lasting split into two lines of the house, with Duke Ludwig IV (1282-1347) retaining the duchy of Bavaria (the Bavarian line) but ceding the Palatinate (the Palatine line) to the descendants of his elder brother, Rudolf the Stammerer (1274-1319).

The Treaty of Pavia provided that in the event of one line of the house dying out, the other line would inherit. This provision would fall in four hundred and forty-eight years later when the Bavarian line became extinct.

In its early days Trausnitz was the residence and centre of government of the newly-created dukes of Bavaria. In 1235, Duke Otto II the Illustrious (son of Ludwig I) received the Emperor Friedrich II (grandson of Friedrich Barbarossa) as his guest here. Friedrich had spent large parts of his life in the Mediterranean and the Middle East and caused a sensation when he entered the town of Landshut with Saracens, elephants, and camels in his train[1]. Friedrich II's son Konrad (later Emperor Konrad IV) married Otto II's daughter, Elisabeth, and their only son, Konradin, was brought up in Bavaria. Duke Konradin of Swabia was the last of the Hohenstaufen line that had provided several Holy Roman emperors. The widowed Elisabeth was living at Trausnitz when she heard the terrible news of Konradin's defeat in battle, capture and execution at Naples in 1268. He was only sixteen-years-old.

42. The crucifix and sculptures in St George's chapel date from around 1230.

St George's Chapel at Trausnitz is one of the original buildings from the early thirteenth century and retains much of its medieval gothic appearance. Fortunately the chapel wing was not damaged by the 1961 fire. The carved crucifix and plaster sculptures on the frieze along the balustrade were made around 1230 and described by our tour guide as 'the amazing treasure' of this schloss. We were delighted to discover that he spoke English and, better still, was willing to do the tour in half-and-half German and English because there was only one other visitor. I was grateful since there was no English guidebook and the English handout for the tour was rudimentary and (I thought) dull.

The heyday of Trausnitz was during the fifteenth century when, after one of the divisions of Wittelsbach lands, it was the capital of the separate state of Bavaria-Landshut. There were four ruling dukes during the one-hundred-year history of this state (1392-1503) and, because of their wealth and power, they are known collectively as *the Rich Dukes* (please see chart 9 for a family tree). Ludwig the Rich had far more money in his treasury than the Holy Roman emperor and wielded so much influence politically that he could arrange a great match for his son with a king's daughter. In 1475 Ludwig's son, Georg the Rich, married Princess Hedwig, the daughter of King Kasimir IV of Poland. There is a gorgeous portrait of Hedwig at Trausnitz, in which she is bedecked with jewellery and wears a gown and headdress studded with precious stones. The marriage of his heir was the zenith of Ludwig's reign and he spared no expense on an ostentatious celebrity wedding. The guest list was a who's who of German royalty and the cost of the week-long festivities was said to amount to Ludwig's total annual income[2]. This wedding has become so famous that it is still re-enacted in Landshut today.

Every fourth year the town of Landshut stages a pageant called the Landshuter Hochzeit 1475 (the 1475 Landshut Wedding). For the forty-first staging in 2017 more than two thousand participants in medieval costume re-enacted a series of events from the real wedding. These include the entry

43. Duke Ludwig the Rich had more money in his treasury than the Holy Roman emperor.

of Princess Hedwig into Landshut after her two month journey from Krakow, escorted by Polish nobles and a long train of wagons carrying her dowry; the tournament in which her bridegroom took part to show off his knightly skills; and the wedding ball in the Town Hall, where Emperor Friedrich III opened the dancing with the bride. Ten thousand guests flocked into Landshut and caroused at the wedding in

1475; modern visitors can enjoy a medieval get-together in Trausnitz with magicians, fire-eaters, jugglers, flag-bearers, music and dancing. There is even a medieval tavern! Beer is very important in Bavaria and Duke Georg the Rich left a lasting legacy when he formulated his famous edict on the purity of Bavarian beer, which I understand is still adhered to today. He said that no other ingredients may be used, apart from malt, hops, yeast and water[3]!

After *the Rich Dukes* died out in the male line, Bavaria-Landshut reverted to dukes of Bavaria-Munich and Trausnitz became a secondary residence. The last high point in its history was the years when Wilhelm

44. An old postcard of the courtyard showing the multi-story renaissance arcades.

V held his court here as crown prince, between his marriage to Renata of Lorraine in 1568 and succeeding his father as duke in 1579. Wilhelm splashed out a lot of money to transform Trausnitz into a magnificent palace in the renaissance style. He was a collector of rare and exotic items and the schloss houses a museum called the *Chamber of Curiosities and Art*, based on the idea of the collection he amassed. Wilhelm's squander-mania style of living at Trausnitz got him into trouble with his father after he had to confess the huge size of his debts to Fugger, the bankers[4]. When fire swept through the Fürstenbau in October 1961, Wilhelm's renaissance interiors were lost – except for a small building called the Italian Annexe which, fortunately, was relatively untouched.

The Italian Annexe is a small rectangular extension to the Fürstenbau with one room on each floor (called a Cabinet) and a narrow winding staircase. Wilhelm V built the annex around 1575 and had it exquisitely painted and decorated by Italian artists and craftsman. The Cabinets are stunning, particularly the vaulted and coffered ceilings, but it was the cramped staircase that was the highlight of Trausnitz for me. It's too precious to allow visitors to climb the stairs, but we could peer in on each floor. Called the Narrentreppe (Fools' or Jesters' Staircase) it is painted with life-sized characters and boisterous scenes from the early form of Italian theatre called *Commedia dell'arte*.

Wilhelm and Renata enjoyed performances of *Commedia dell'arte* during their wedding celebrations and kept a troop of actors permanently at their court. After one performance a courtier wrote (translated) 'we laughed so hard we peed our pants'[5]. This style of theatre is a mixture of comedy, slapstick, and farce. The plot has stock characters but no fixed script; the actors improvise along a storyline. The paintings on the Narrentreppe feature the antics of an elderly merchant called Pantalone and his servant Zanni. They romp up and down the staircase – Pantalone rides a donkey up while Zanni tries to give the poor animal an enema; Pantalone fights Zanni and throws him down the stairs, a bare-bosomed woman empties a chamber pot over both of them from an upstairs window. The Fools' staircase is a delightful oddity but very lowbrow and uncouth, and seems an unlikely subject for the formality and gravity of a prince's court; particularly since Wilhelm V underwent a personality change during his years at Trausnitz and became religious and sober. He spent his last years living as a hermit (see Schleissheim later in this chapter) and is known in history as Duke Wilhelm the Pious! If you would like to see the Fools' Staircase but can't get to Trausnitz, take a look at the schloss website (www.burg-trausnitz.de/englisch) where there is a virtual tour.

After Wilhelm V, Trausnitz was rarely used as a royal residence and suffered centuries of decline. The Swedes took the castle in 1634, during the Thirty Years War, and some of the fortifications were blown up. In the eighteenth century it was used as a military barracks and later as a woollen and silk factory; in the nineteenth century it was an isolation hospital for cholera; in the twentieth a store for state archives. King Ludwig II of Bavaria had a suite of rooms in the Fürstenbau fitted out in the 1870s but he never stayed in them and they too were lost to the 1961 fire. A small exhibition in these rooms has photographs of how they used to look.

The tour ends in a large covered balcony called the Söller, twenty metres up on the second floor, which is thought to date back to *the Rich Dukes*. This is an open-air entertaining space with a stage for musicians at one end and an outside staircase at the other leading directly to the kitchens so food could be brought up. From here we had a great view of the town of Landshut and the prominent steeple of St Martin's church (one hundred and thirty-one metres high and the tallest brick-built steeple in the world). The church is on the main street, called Altstadt, where there is a second schloss, called Landshut Residence.

Landshut Residence

Landshut Residence is in the centre of the old town of Landshut, opposite the town hall on Altstadt. It was built by Wilhelm V's great uncle Ludwig X between 1536 and 1543. Ludwig was the younger brother of Duke Wilhelm IV of Bavaria (see chart 9) and, because the brothers were born before their father's decree of primogeniture (inheritance by the eldest son) in 1506, they ruled jointly. (It was fortuitous that Ludwig had no heir so that the primogeniture rule took effect after his death.) Ludwig was the governor of Landshut and first of all lived at Trausnitz. But he thought this old schloss was outdated and built a new one in the town.

Ludwig X's palace is well camouflaged and hard to spot. This is because the front wing (called the German building) is hidden behind a façade that was added two hundred and fifty years later in a different style. This blends in so well with the other buildings on Altstadt it is hard to pick out. But behind the German building is a renaissance palace called the Italian building with an attractive arcaded courtyard and beautiful painted and plasterwork interiors. This was the first palace built in renaissance style north of the Alps and was inspired by a palazzo in Mantua that Ludwig had visited on his Italian travels.

Burghausen

Burghausen proudly proclaims itself as the longest castle in Europe. We stopped at a vantage point, some distance away, and could see a line of buildings stretching all the way down the skyline on top of a steep wooded ridge. Which part is the schloss I wondered? And the answer is – all of it! From the entrance at one end to the duke's palace at the other is a distance of more than a kilometre[6].

Burghausen is located in the far east of Upper Bavaria, right at the border with Austria. The site is picturesque, on the top of a long narrow rocky ridge between two stretches of water (see the hand-drawn sketch map). The milky waters of the river Salzach flow in a curve along the east and south sides of the schloss, with the town of Burghausen clinging to a narrow strip of land between the river and the castle ridge. On the west side of the ridge is a lake called the Wöhrsee that was left behind when the river changed its course in the Ice Age. The top of the ridge is elongated and narrow and there are marvellous views out from the schloss in all directions.

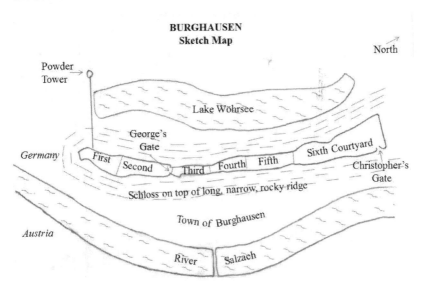

BURGHAUSEN
Sketch Map

North

Powder Tower

Lake Wöhrsee

George's Gate

Germany

First Second Third Fourth Fifth Sixth Courtyard

Christopher's Gate

Schloss on top of long, narrow, rocky ridge

Town of Burghausen

Austria

River Salzach

This is a schloss with a difference because Burghausen is a whole jumble of buildings built in six connecting sections, called courtyards, down the full length of the ridge. From the entrance in the Sixth Courtyard, at the northern end of the site, we walked through four more courtyards to reach the First Courtyard at the southern end, with the most important buildings. There was plenty of material in English for a self-guided tour of this open-air museum, and my only problem initially was that the information board in each courtyard numbered them differently from the English guidebook. Once I worked this out I really enjoyed my visit and we were here for an awfully long time!

45. Burghausen was the border fortress of the dukes of Bavaria-Landshut.

Burghausen was a secondary residence of the dukes of Bavaria-Landshut and is particularly associated with Duke Georg the Rich (1455-1503) and his Polish wife Hedwig (1457-1502) who moved here after their famous wedding in Landshut in 1475 (see Trausnitz above). Their coats of arms hang over George's Gate (Georgstor) between the Second and Third Courtyards. It used to be thought that their marriage must have been unhappy because Duchess Hedwig stayed on at Burghausen when, after he became the duke, her husband moved to Trausnitz. But it is clear that Georg maintained his wife and children in great style at Burghausen and made frequent visits – so perhaps Hedwig just liked living here. She died at Burghausen in 1502.

The Bavarian line

The Bavarian line of the house of Wittelsbach divided into branches in 1392 to provide separate states for brothers. The branch of Bavaria-Ingolstadt was notable for providing a queen of France (Queen Isabeau (1370-1435) wife of King Charles VI), but died out in 1447, leaving just two branches in the Bavarian line – Bavaria-Landshut and Bavaria-Munich.

The death of the last duke of Bavaria-Landshut in 1503 sparked a fraternal war in the house. The Landshut War of Succession (1504-05) was decided in favour of Bavaria-Munich so that the separate branches of the Bavarian line were now reunited into a single duchy of Bavaria.

In a smart move, Duke Albrecht IV of Bavaria (known as the Wise) then introduced the rule of primogeniture in 1506, so in future the duchy would descend intact to the eldest son and there were no more divisions of the inheritance on this side of the House. The Bavarian line of the house of Wittelsbach became extinct on the death of Elector Maximilian III Joseph in 1777 (see Nymphenburg later in this chapter), when – in accordance with the Treaty of Pavia – the inheritance went to the Palatine line.

After Georg succeeded his father in 1479, he spent enormous amounts on a building programme to modernise Burghausen as a residence for his family and also turn it into the strongest fortress in Europe. Up to four thousand craftsmen and labourers were working here at any one time[7]. Georg was concerned to protect his state from a Turkish invasion coming from the east (a real threat since the fall of Constantinople to the Turks in 1453) and also wanted a secure place to store his valuables. The treasure of the rich dukes was famous among their contemporaries and when it had to be moved after Georg's death it took seventy wagons, each drawn by six horses, to transport the haul[8]! The source of their great wealth came from agricultural levies on the grain production in their state and from customs duties on the salt trade on the river Salzach (the waters are milky because of the salt deposits). Salt was known as *white gold* and until 1594 Burghausen enjoyed a monopoly on all the salt coming into Bavaria.

Georg's problem was that both his sons had died as babies and the only surviving children of his marriage to Hedwig were two daughters. The elder (Elisabeth) was married to Rupprecht of the Palatine (from the Palatine line of the house), and the younger (Margarethe) became a religious abbess. There was a family agreement that if Bavaria-Landshut died out in the male line, its territory would be inherited by Bavaria-Munich. But Georg tried to circumvent this by leaving his state to Elisabeth and her husband. The result was a war of succession after he died in 1503. The emperor took the side of Bavaria-Munich and the two duchies (which had split in 1392) were reunited. Elisabeth and Rupprecht both died of disease during the war, but as part of the peace a small new duchy was created for their two young sons (see Neuburg later in this chapter).

46. Georgstor (George's Gate) with the coats of arms of Duke Georg the Rich and his wife Princess Hedwig of Poland.

Christopher's Gate (Christophstor) into the Sixth (or outermost) courtyard was the main entrance to Burghausen and the old steep road still leads down to the town from here. This is the largest courtyard and has the feeling of a village, with a cluster of buildings on either side of a main street running down the middle. After the Landshut War of Succession the enlarged new duchy of Bavaria was split into four administrative districts and Burghausen became a district centre. Government functions were based in the schloss and the names of the buildings in this courtyard show which officials lived and worked here – Forester's Tower, Chimney Sweep's Tower, Tax Clerk's Office ... .

Hedwig's Chapel in the Fifth Courtyard was built by Duke Georg and Duchess Hedwig and inaugurated in 1489. One end of the chapel forms part of the fortifications so that an unusual feature is the loopholes in the chapel wall for defenders to fire from. On the other side of this courtyard are tremendous views down to the Wöhrsee and to the circular Powder Tower built by Georg the Rich in 1488 (where gunpowder was stored well away from the main schloss). This exposed barbican was the first line of defence and is linked to the main fortifications by a long wall. The Powder Tower has walls five metres thick and its own well, so the garrison could hold out.

The buildings in the Fourth Courtyard include the Witches' Tower, Prison, and Torture Tower. In the eighteenth century Burghausen became a military garrison and was also used as a prison. The small Witches Tower was a death cell for serious female offenders and in the short years between 1748 and 1776, eleven hundred death sentences were carried out here – so many that 'Burghausen was likened throughout Bavaria to a knacker's yard'[9]! The original instruments were still in the Torture Tower until 1918 when it became private residential accommodation. Today the tower houses a privately-owned museum of torture and a small shop.

A charming feature of the Third Courtyard is the row of three small octagonal look-out towers, called the *Pepper Castors* because of their shape and tall pointed roofs. The swallow-tail battlements on the armoury are known colloquially as *Oath Fingers* (Schwurfinger) because of the practice of raising a thumb and two fingers to swear allegiance to the emperor. George's Gate, at the narrowest point of the ridge, guards the entrance to the second courtyard. The views from here are the best in the entire castle. When Napoleon visited Burghausen in April 1809 he watched from here as French army engineers built a pontoon bridge over the Salzach to replace that destroyed by the retreating Austrians. He came with an army of one hundred thousand men and when they left, four days later, the town was faced with famine!

47. The fortified First Courtyard.

In the Second Courtyard the old brewery is now a café and, by the time we got here, we were ready for a break. With the First Courtyard this was part of the restricted area of the inner castle – the punishment for being found in here without permission was to have your ears cut off! And finally, after a walk of one kilometre, we reached the First Courtyard at the other end of the complex. This is the smallest of the six courtyards and also the best defended, being surrounded by a deep moat and massive walls. Ludwig the Concealed (he wore a beard), the troublesome duke of Bavaria-Ingolstadt, died while imprisoned in the Keep (the Bergfried) in the First Courtyard in 1447. Around the small internal courtyard are the most important buildings of the ducal court. The Duke's Palace (Palas) and the Ladies Bower (Kemenate) are now both museums, and the court common room (Dürnitz) is the ticket office.

We saw the duke's apartments in the Palas, where Georg the Rich stayed on his visits to Duchess Hedwig. Also on display in the Palas were six monumental paintings depicting events (real or imagined) in the history of the Bavarian line. These huge and dynamic pictures were painted by the court artist Hans Werl between 1601 and 1603 for Duke Maximilian I. They are jam-packed with action, extremely detailed, and good fun to look at. One shows the victory of Ludwig the Rich of Bavaria-Landshut (the father of Georg) at the battle of Giengen in 1462 (over the margrave of Brandenburg). The captured canon and other loot were brought to Burghausen.

Burghausen was the great border fortress of Bavaria and its decline began in 1800 when Napoleon ordered the disabling of its defences, so that the schloss could not be used against him. Around twenty kilometres upstream on the river Salzach (to the south), our next schloss was the border fortress for another state of the Holy Roman Empire – called the Archbishopric of Salzburg.

Burg Tittmoning

48. Burg Tittmoning in the area of Bavaria called *Rupertiwinkel.*

Tittmoning is in the delightfully named *Rupertiwinkel*. This is a small area of Upper Bavaria which in the Holy Roman Empire was part of a church state called the Archbishopric of Salzburg. The name *Rupertiwinkel* was invented at the end of the nineteenth century and comes from St Rupert, who was the first bishop of Salzburg. When the Empire was dissolved, the area became part of the Archduchy of Austria and later, when the boundary with Austria was redrawn at the Salzach River in 1816 (after the Napoleonic Wars), the *Rupertiwinkel* was incorporated into the kingdom of Bavaria[10].

I had never heard of Burg Tittmoning before my visit, and we only found it when driving past on our way to somewhere else. Just outside the town of Tittmoning, on top of a steep hill, we spotted an old castle with massive white stone walls topped at one end by a distinctive red-tiled pitched roof (this is a grain store called the Troadkasten, built in 1553). Which noble family had this schloss belonged to, I wondered? When we walked up the hill to take a look, things became more curious

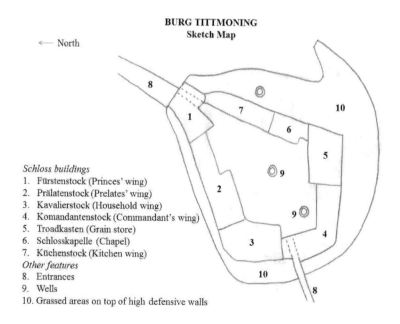

BURG TITTMONING
Sketch Map

←— North

Schloss buildings
1. Fürstenstock (Princes' wing)
2. Prälatenstock (Prelates' wing)
3. Kavalierstock (Household wing)
4. Komandantenstock (Commandant's wing)
5. Troadkasten (Grain store)
6. Schlosskapelle (Chapel)
7. Küchenstock (Kitchen wing)
Other features
8. Entrances
9. Wells
10. Grassed areas on top of high defensive walls

as the road to the schloss is called Pope Benedict XVI Way. What could be the connection between the first pope to retire from the job and a small castle on the eastern border of Germany? Of course – he was the German Cardinal Ratzinger who was elected Pope in 2005 and resigned in 2013. We found out later

49. The Burg is protected by a deep rift and the only entrance is by drawbridge.

that Pope Benedict was born nearby and as a child spent several years living in the town of Tittmoning with his family. I much enjoyed my visit to this surprising schloss and finding out its history.

Burg Tittmoning was acquired in 1234 by Archbishop of Salzburg Eberhard II von Regensburg (reigned 1200-1246) in response to the growing power of his neighbours. The Archbishopric of Salzburg was sandwiched between the Duchy of Bavaria to the west and the Archduchy of Austria to the east, and Burg Tittmoning was a border fortress against these larger and more powerful states. The site of the castle, on top of a high rocky outcrop and next to a deep rift, meant that it could only be entered by the drawbridges and was thought to be virtually impregnable. But over the following centuries, in the course of disputes between these three adjoining territories, it would be taken by Bavaria several times.

Duke Ludwig IV of Bavaria took Tittmoning by subterfuge in 1324, after it was betrayed and the town gates opened. Ludwig was the elected Holy Roman emperor; but a rival (Austrian Hapsburg) emperor had also been elected by a different faction and the archbishop of Salzburg was in the rival's camp[11]. Ludwig destroyed the Burg and plundered the town, and then sold them both back to the archbishop in 1327 at an inflated price[12]. In 1611 Duke Maximilian of Bavaria took the Burg by force during a war with the archbishop over the production of salt; when he got it back in 1614, the archbishop had to repair extensive damage[13]. And the troops of a Bavarian Holy Roman emperor were at Burg Tittmoning again in 1743, when they plundered the grain store during the War of the Austrian Succession[14].

Burg Tittmoning fell for the last time during the Napoleonic Wars when French troops occupied the schloss and set fire to the gatehouse on 16 December 1805. Several buildings burned down, including the Fürstenstock (Princes' Wing) that housed the archbishops' apartments. The Archbishopric of Salzburg no longer existed (because of secularisation) so there was little interest in rebuilding what had been destroyed. Parts of Burg Tittmoning were sold off privately and the municipal poorhouse moved into the Kavalierstock (household wing). Eventually, in 1851, the city of Tittmoning bought what was left, in an attempt to stop the rot[15]. During World War II the schloss was a prisoner of war camp and afterwards a transit camp for refugees fleeing from the Soviet army.

50. View of the courtyard and the chapel built by Archbishop von Thun.

Laufen

The schloss at Laufen on the river Salzach was a summer residence of the archbishops of Salzburg. I had heard of it before my visit because of a lady in my village in Cornwall, Great Britain. As a child, Gloria was one of many hundreds of civilians who were deported from the island of Jersey in the Channel Islands in September 1942, on the direct orders of Hitler, and sent to spend the war in captivity in Germany.

Ten-year-old Gloria, with her parents, younger sisters and brother, spent three years interned in the schloss at Wurzach in Baden-Wurttemberg; another sister was born there. (I hope to include Schloss Wurzach in a future book.) The single men from the Channel Islands were sent to Laufen. This had been a prisoner-of-war camp called Oflag VII-C for British officers captured on the

fall of France, with an offshoot in Burg Tittmoning. Now Laufen became an internment camp for civilians but remained under military control.

Nowadays there is not a lot to see at Schloss Laufen and I didn't find anyone who knew its history. The main building is an office block and the supplementary building (behind it) looked to be private apartments. I liked the clock tower (on the left in the illustration) that leads to an arresting metalwork bridge across the Salzach into Austria, with sculptures of eagles coming in to land on the top span.

Today Burg Tittmoning has been restored and is a curious mixture of historical monument and residential street. Our visit was on Monday (when the museums in the schloss were closed) but fortunately there was an information board in the courtyard. The Rupertiwinkel museum of local history occupies the Kavalierstock; there is a Tannery museum (tannery is the production of leather) in the Troadkasten; and the museum café is in the Prälatenstock (Prelates Wing). (Please see the hand-drawn sketch map on page 96 which explains the layout and gives the names of the buildings.) But other parts of the Burg are family homes; a sign on the Kitchen Wing (Küchenstock), which has pretty window boxes and a flowerbed of pink roses, showed that this has been in private ownership since 1815.

The chapel at Burg Tittmoning was rebuilt by Archbishop of Salzburg Johann Ernst von Thun in 1693-1694. He had two new bells cast for the bell-tower and also commissioned the magnificent altar painting by Johann Michael Rottmayr, which is the masterpiece of this schloss. The chapel is dedicated to St Michael and the altar painting shows the archangel Michael throwing the devil (the fallen angel Lucifer) out of heaven. Rottmayr was a local artist (he came from Laufen – see page 99) who trained in Venice and also painted the ceilings in the archbishops' main residence in Salzburg. As the church was locked I have only seen this painting as a reproduction in a book, but it looks to be a lovely thing, full of movement and colour[16].

Before driving on we stopped in the town of Tittmoning to visit the information office. This intriguing little town still has its medieval layout with narrow fortified gates at either end of a long (two hundred and ninety-eight metres) town square shaped like a trapezoid. An enthusiastic

51. The house where Pope Benedict XVI lived as a child.

assistant helped with information in English about the Burg and also showed us the house where Pope Benedict lived as a child. His father was a police officer and the family moved around according to his postings. The young Joseph Ratzinger (born 1927) lived here between 1929 and 1932 and attended kindergarten school. They are very proud in Tittmoning of this local son.

Neuburg

Neuburg on the Danube was the capital of a principality called Palatine (or Pfalz)-Neuburg, ruled by the Palatine line of the house of Wittelsbach. The view below, taken from the river bank, shows the huge East Wing of the schloss, built by the sixth duke of Palatine-Neuburg in the 1660s. The reason I wanted to come here is because that wing houses a museum about the history of this little state which, by the hand of fate, would be the cradle of the Bavarian kings. In the survivor-take-all system of inheritance in the house of Wittelsbach, it was a descendant of a duke of Palatine-Neuburg who became the first king of Bavaria on 1 January 1806.

52. Schloss Neuburg on the River Danube.

There were nine dukes from the foundation of the Neuburg principality in 1505 until it became a province of Bavaria in 1799 (all shown in chart 10). The museum has a room devoted to each, with key information, portraits and other artefacts. I liked the logical progression of this layout and how it highlighted the difference in style and dress between the generations. The problem for me was that none of the information was translated into English. I decided to take photos and make copious notes to translate when I got home; but my rapid scribbling aroused the suspicion of a museum attendant who silently tracked me from room to room. I tried to explain what I was up to, but we had a language barrier between us!

The first duke of Palatine-Neuburg was Ottheinrich (1502-1559). He

has an unusual name which I saw spelt four different ways while researching this book[17]. Ottheinrich is one of the larger-than-life characters in the house of Wittelsbach and has been called the Bavarian Henry VIII. I think this comparison is apt – the two men were contemporaries; both were at the centre of a splendid court; both introduced the Protestant Reformation to their countries; and both had the problem of no son. They even look alike in their portraits, especially in later life when they both grew extremely large. Palatine-Neuburg was created for

53. Duke Ottheinrich of Palatine-Neuburg has been called the Bavarian Henry VIII.

Ottheinrich and his younger brother when they were toddlers, following a bloody war of succession between branches of the house.

The Palatine line

The Palatine line dates from the division of the house of Wittelsbach under the Treaty of Pavia of 1329. They were rulers of the Palatine, a separate state in the Holy Roman Empire with lands along the Rhine called the Lower Palatinate, and in the Upper Palatinate in Bavaria. The Treaty of Pavia envisioned that the right to vote in the election of a Holy Roman emperor would alternate between the Bavarian and Palatine lines of the house, but the Golden Bull of 1356 (regulating elections) confirmed the Palatine in this position.

The Palatine line went through several divisions into different branches, so that their family tree looks like a spider's web (see chart 8). The senior of the branches was the Heidelberg branch but this became extinct in 1559 on the death of Ottheinrich. He was succeeded in Heidelberg by the Simmern branch of the Palatine line, but as duke of Palatine-Neuburg by Duke Wolfgang from the (more junior) Zweibrücken branch.

The Simmern were Calvinist and at the start of the Thirty Years War (1618-1648), Friedrich V risked all to accept the throne of Bohemia in direct opposition to the Catholic Holy Roman emperor. The gamble did not pay off; Friedrich lost both Bohemia and the Palatine and spent the rest of his life in exile. He is known as the Winter King because his rule in Bohemia lasted only one winter. His prestigious role as prince-elector was also taken away and given to the Bavarian line in 1623. But in the peace treaty that followed the war, an extra vote was created for Friedrich V's son, who was also restored to the Lower Palatinate but had to cede the Upper Palatinate to Bavaria.

After the Simmern branch died out in 1685, the Palatine was inherited in turn by branches descended from Duke Wolfgang of Zweibrücken. The inheritance went first to the New Neuburg branch and, when this died out in 1742, to Karl Theodor of the Sulzbach branch. Karl Theodor was the beneficiary of the Treaty of Pavia when the Bavarian line became extinct in 1777 and, after four hundred and forty-eight years, the two sides of the house of Wittelsbach were reunited. When Karl Theodor himself died without an heir in 1799, the inheritance passed to the Birkenfeld-Zweibrücken branch of the Palatine line.

Ottheinrich was the son of Elisabeth of Bavaria-Landshut and her husband, Rupprecht of the Palatine. After the death of his grandfather, Duke Georg the Rich of Bavaria-Landshut (Elisabeth's father) in 1503, his parents went to war over her inheritance (please see Burghausen above for the Landshut War of Succession). Both parents died during the war and the cause was lost. But under the peace agreement of 1505, some scattered lands were pieced together into a small new duchy for the orphaned Ottheinrich, aged three, and his younger brother[18].

As a young man, Ottheinrich helped to mend the family breach by marrying the daughter of the duke of Bavaria who had gone to war with his parents. Susanna of Bavaria (see chart 9) was a widow and came with five children from her first marriage[19]. She suffered two miscarriages as the wife of Ottheinrich but there were no children[20]. Unlike Henry VIII, Ottheinrich did not try to get rid of her to marry again; he solved his problem by gifting Palatine-Neuburg to a distant cousin as his successor.

Entrance to Neuburg is through a tunnel in the west wing and into the internal courtyard. From the outside, views of the schloss are

54. The internal courtyard showing the north and west wings (middle and left) built by Ottheinrich.

dominated by the huge East Wing overlooking the river Danube, built in baroque style by Duke Philipp Wilhelm of Palatine-Neuburg in the 1660s. Outside the ticket office are quirky stone statues of Philipp and his wife (Anna of Jülich, Kleve and Berg), dating from 1661. But in the courtyard, it is the three wings built by Ottheinrich in the 1530s that catch the eye.

The North and South Wings have the distinctive renaissance gables that are one of my favourite architectural features, and the West Wing (or Ottheinrich Building) houses the first-ever Protestant church. The decoration of this chapel is quite plain apart from the gallery and ceiling, which are covered by a colourful cycle of more than forty religious pictures, painted by Hans Bocksberger in 1543. The largest painting shows the Ascension of Christ up to heaven, accompanied by angels and watched from below by his astonished disciples. The artist has tried to get the perspective right and I looked up at the figure of Christ and the angels from the soles of their naked feet. The façade of the West Wing is decorated with sgraffito paintings by the Dutch master Hans Schroer. These were commissioned in the 1560s by Ottheinrich's successor. The sgraffito technique involves scratching lines through layers of plaster to reveal the image underneath.

Ottheinrich lavished money on his schloss, seriously overreaching himself as he transformed it into a grand renaissance palace where he lived in extravagant style. And this caused him problems when, in 1542, he declared publically for the new Lutheran faith and Palatine-Neuburg became Protestant. His wife Susanna's brother, Duke Wilhelm IV of Bavaria, was appalled by Ottheinrich's conversion. In the religious disputes that would now convulse the Holy Roman Empire, the Bavarian line of the house of Wittelsbach remained staunchly Catholic, while the Palatine line was mostly Protestant. Wilhelm IV had been financing his brother-in-law's life style but now withdrew his line of credit. Overburdened by his debts, Ottheinrich went bankrupt and was forced into exile from Neuburg in 1544. Two years later, his schloss was captured and plundered by troops of the Catholic Emperor Karl V as he tried to suppress the Protestant territories during the Schmalkaldic Wars of religion (1546-1547). These wars were named after the town of Schmalkalden in Thuringia where the Protestant princes met to establish a military alliance (see Wilhelmsburg in *Schloss III*). Ottheinrich did not return to Neuburg until 1552.

Towards the end of his life, in 1556, Ottheinrich succeeded an uncle (his father's brother) as ruler of the Palatine (a much bigger state) and moved to its capital of Heidelberg. He had already chosen Duke Wolfgang (1526-1569) from the Zweibrücken branch of the house of Wittelsbach as his successor in Neuburg and gifted him the principality on the condition it stayed Lutheran[21]. Wolfgang would be the progenitor of the Bavarian kings, but I will always associate Schloss Neuburg with its first duke – the colourful Ottheinrich, Bavaria's Henry VIII.

Schleissheim

55. Elector Maximilian II Emanuel.

Schleissheim is a monument to the self-aggrandisement of an ambitious Elector of Bavaria. The schloss is a complex of three separate palaces linked together in a linear axis of gardens and canals, and two of them were built by Elector Maximilian II Emanuel (1662-1726). The star of this prince rose high and he had ambitions to the throne of Spain, and to supplant the Hapsburgs and become Holy Roman emperor. But pride can come before a fall. After a disastrous defeat at the Battle of Blenheim, Max Emanuel (as he is usually known) was forced into exile and Schleissheim never became the imperial capital that he intended. And Max Emanuel's policy of not permitting his younger sons to get married, to keep the inheritance of the Bavarian line of the house of

56. The New Palace at Schleissheim is a monument to Max Emanuel's victories in the Turkish wars.

Wittelsbach intact, would backfire when this line became extinct on the death of his grandson.

The history of Schleissheim began modestly in 1597 when Duke Wilhelm V, known as the Pious, purchased a farm north of Munich. Wilhelm was a lavish spender, as we have already seen at Trausnitz, and apparently saw no conflict between this and his piety. When Bavaria was teetering on the verge of bankruptcy, he abdicated in 1598 in favour of his son and retreated to his new property. Wilhelm built eight chapels in the area, each with a hermit's cell attached, and spent the last twenty-seven-years of his life living in seclusion in two simple rooms in the farmhouse, wall-papered in black[22]!

The first of the three palaces at Schleissheim (called the Alte Schloss, or Old Palace) was built as a hunting lodge by Wilhelm's son, Duke Maximilian I, between 1617 and 1623. Maximilian was a leader of the Catholic League of princes and was rewarded by the emperor in 1623 for his victory at the Battle of the White Mountain (1620), with the return of the rank of prince-elector (lost to the Palatine line of the house in 1356). Maximilian I was the first of five electors from the Bavarian line of the house before this line died out (please see chart 11). The Old Palace was destroyed by bombing in World War II and reconstructed in the 1970s. The interior is modern exhibition space; it houses a museum of folklore and a colourful collection of Christmas Cribs from around the world.

Max Emanuel was the grandson of Maximilian I. His successes came young. He succeeded his father at sixteen, and before he was barely out of his teens Max Emanuel was forging a reputation as a military commander, fighting with Emperor Leopold I in the battle of Vienna (1683) against the Turks. In 1685 he married Archduchess Maria Antonia of Austria, Leopold's only surviving child from his first wife. She was a great catch – not only as the daughter of the emperor but because, from her mother, she had a good claim to the throne of Spain. As the son-in-law of the Holy Roman emperor and the nephew-in-law of the childless Carlos II (the last Hapsburg king of Spain), Max Emanuel was riding high. Before he was thirty, he was promoted to be governor of the Spanish Netherlands (parts of modern Belgium, Luxemburg and northern France, then ruled by the king of Spain).

Between 1684 and 1688, Max Emanuel built the second palace, called Lustheim (Pleasure House), one kilometre to the east of the Old Palace, to celebrate his marriage to Maria Antonia. The small

57. Lustheim was built to celebrate Max Emanuel's first marriage to the emperor's daughter.

schloss was surrounded by a canal and accessed only by gondola in an allusion to Cythera, the mythical island of love. Lustheim was the scene of many brilliant balls and court entertainments, including a visit from the emperor in 1690. But in fact Max Emanuel's marriage was unhappy[23]. Maria Antonia died in 1692 after giving birth to their son, Joseph Ferdinand. The little boy was nominated as the heir to Spain but he too died – in 1699, at six years old.

Part of the enjoyment of a visit to Schleissheim is the long walk through the gardens, past the fountains and cascade and down the side of the canal, to see Lustheim. The schloss is home to an important collection of Meissen porcelain but some of the original décor survives, particularly in the impressive central room called the Festival Hall, two stories high. The initials of Max Emanuel and Maria Antonia recur in the decorations here, but the collection of portraits in the hall is all about his second marriage to Theresa Kunigunde, the daughter of King Johann III Sobieski of Poland. The new electress added to the family every year and there are portraits of their eight children born between 1696 and 1703 (a girl and seven boys), all painted by Martin Maingaud in 1703 (another son was born in 1704). These pictures are delightful – seven-year-old Maria Anna Carolina and her six-year-old brother Karl Albrecht wear miniature versions of adult clothes; the younger boys are still in skirts, and baby Johann Theodor is a naked cherub with a garland of flowers. After things went wrong for Max Emanuel in 1704, Theresa Kunigunde lived apart from him for many years.

In 1701, at the height of his career, Max Emanuel laid the foundation stone for a huge new palace at Schleissheim. He felt himself within touching distance of becoming Holy Roman emperor and this was to be his imperial residence, to rival Versailles or Schönbrunn in Vienna. The Neue Schloss (New Palace) is the third palace on the site, built in front of the Old Palace and in a direct line with Lustheim, at the other end of the formal gardens. Max Emanuel's original plan was to incorporate the Old Palace with the New Palace in a massive four-wing structure and this is why the two are so close together. But when he was exiled from Bavaria in 1704 only the shell of a single wing had been started. The elector was forced to simplify his plans. When work resumed in 1719 after his return, the rest was never built.

The New Palace is three hundred metres long, grand, impersonal, empty, and very cold inside. I was advised at the ticket desk to keep my coat on but even so I wished that, like the attendants, I had a woolly hat! Schleissheim was a summer palace and so intended to stay cool, but when we visited on a day in May it was freezing in there. After the death of Max Emanuel, his successors had little use for this monument to his glory; the contents were dispersed to other Wittelsbacher schlösser and in 1836 the New Palace became a picture gallery. It was badly damaged by bombing in World War II but both the building and interiors have been restored.

The rooms of the New Palace are laid out in a long enfilade (single line of connecting rooms) with the ceremonial spaces in the middle (the Grand Staircase, Banqueting Hall, Hall of Victories, and Great Gallery) flanked by the Elector's Apartments on one side and the Electress's on the other. The decoration in most rooms is very macho and a celebration of war, with the theme being Max Emanuel's prowess as a military commander and his victories in the Turkish wars. Tapestries and canvases depict his battles and the ceiling painting in the Great Hall compares his successes to the Olympian gods.

58. The Grand Staircase in the New Palace leads to the Hall of Victories and Banqueting Hall.

Only in the Electress's apartments is the décor more delicate with silver plated stucco and allegories of virtue and peace. These rooms were not fitted out for Max Emanuel's wife, but for his daughter-in-law, Archduchess Maria Amalia of Austria, who married his heir, Karl Albrecht, in 1722[24]. I especially liked the small private chapel at the far end of her rooms (the Kammerkapelle or Chamber Chapel), where

the walls glow with an expensive inlaid material called scagliola (made with glue and coloured dyes) and the unusual ceiling has an open lantern cut through to reveal paintings in the room above. Maria Amalia was permitted this private oratory because of the distance to the palace chapel at the other end of the enfilade.

Everything went pear-shaped for Max Emanuel in the War of the Spanish Succession (1701-1714) about who should succeed Carlos II of Spain. He hoped to push his own candidacy by siding with Louis XIV

59. Dining Hall with equestrian portrait of Max Emanuel.

of France and opposing the Hapsburg emperor. But Max Emanuel was defeated by the emperor's English allies at the battle of Blenheim (called the battle of Höchstädt in Germany) in 1704 and ended up an exile in France. The family were split up for more than a decade, with his sons as hostages in Austria and their mother, Theresa Kunigunde, in Venice. Max Emanuel said that during these sad years his only joy was planning future building projects[25]. His return to Bavaria in 1715, after the war had ended, was marked by a frenzy of building activity – not just at Schleissheim but also at Nymphenburg and Dachau (see over, and Fürstenried (chapter 6). This elector left a mountain of debt and it took his successors almost a hundred years to recover[26]. The idea to transfer the capital of Bavaria from Munich to Schleissheim was shelved.

Dachau

Schloss Dachau is just twenty minutes by car from Schleissheim. The name Dachau is inextricably associated with the atrocities of the Nazi concentration camp and this must never be forgotten. But the town and the schloss today are an attractive place to visit.

Schloss Dachau was once a summer residence of the dukes of Bavaria. During the reigns of Duke Wilhelm IV (1493-1550) and Duke Albrecht V

(1528-1579), the old castle on the site was transformed into a four-wing renaissance palace, including a first floor banqueting hall with a magnificent carved wooden ceiling and a walled garden. After his return to Bavaria from exile in 1715, Elector Maximilian II Emanuel remodelled the schloss in baroque style and added a grand new staircase up to the hall. But after him Dachau fell on hard times. During the Napoleonic Wars the schloss was occupied by French troops and after the wars it was in such bad condition that three of the four wings were knocked down, leaving only the wing with the banqueting hall standing.

Today, the ground floor of Schloss Dachau is a café and restaurant with a terrace in the walled garden and a panoramic view which, on a clear day, goes as far as the Alps. This is the place to have lunch or a snack and then, in a most unusual arrangement, you can buy an entrance ticket from the waiter or waitress and climb the stairs to see the banqueting hall with its wonderful renaissance ceiling (1564-1566). The hall also has a delightful frieze with portraits of the gods and their defining accoutrements – Neptune with his trident, Pan with pipes, Saturn a scythe, Venus with cupid's arrow, and Vulcan with a sledge-hammer. Dachau is well worth the trip.

Nymphenburg

Joyous Nymphenburg was the summer residence of the electors of Bavaria. We visited the schloss on a holiday weekend when all of Munich seemed to be at Nymphenburg, dressed in Bavarian costume or Sunday best. There were brides having their photographs taken in the luxuriant Stone Hall, a gondola plying the central canal in the gardens, and plenty of beer being served in the café in the Palm House. Everyone – from museum attendants to the ladies in the café – was relaxed and friendly. It was a happy place and great fun to visit. This schloss was a favourite with the Bavarian electors and Duke Franz (the current head of house Wittelsbach) still has his home in a wing of the palace. I was told he is often seen strolling through the gardens, although I didn't spot him on my visit. (Please see chart 11 for the Bavarian electors of the house of Wittelsbach.)

60. Nymphenburg was the summer palace of the electors of Bavaria.

Nymphenburg was built in celebration of the birth of a longed-for heir to Bavaria. In 1662 Electress Henriette Adelaide gave birth to her son (the future Max Emanuel) after ten years of marriage. In gratitude, Elector Ferdinand Maria (1636-1679) gave his wife a huge piece of land outside Munich and the electress built a cube-shaped schloss on the site reminiscent of the villas of her northern Italian homeland. Henriette Adelaide was a princess of Savoy and grew up in the cultured and fun-loving court of Turin. She was intelligent, lively, and outspoken, and suffered a culture shock when she arrived in the strict and pious Munich court as a sixteen-year-old to marry Ferdinand Maria. She wasn't much impressed with her sixteen-year-old husband either and her pro-French views (her mother was a sister of Louis XIII so Henriette Adelaide was a first cousin of Louis XIV) caused conflict between the couple. The marriage reached crisis point in 1657, when Ferdinand Maria refused an offer (sponsored by France) of the throne of the Holy Roman Empire, out of concern for the interests of the Austrian Hapsburgs[27]. After the birth of Max Emanuel, Henriette Adelaide's position improved and she is credited with initiating the pleasure-loving culture of the later electors' court and being a big influence on her son.

61. The *Gallery of Beauties* at Nymphenburg, created by King Ludwig I;
his daughter-in-law, Marie of Prussia, on the left,
his mistress, Lola Montez, on the right.

King Ludwig I's Gallery of Beauties in Nymphenburg

The famous Gallery of Beauties in Nymphenburg is a collection of thirty-six portraits of beautiful women commissioned by King Ludwig I (1786-1868) between 1827 and 1850. Ludwig was a notorious ladies man and admirer of feminine beauty. His marriage to Queen Therese was successful and affectionate, but only because the long-suffering queen tolerated his affairs and absences and generally did not make a fuss. Ludwig assured his wife that 'However many hundreds, even thousands of women I have seen, I know none that I could compare to my Therese[28]*'. The subjects Ludwig chose came from all walks of life – from his daughter-in-law, Princess Marie of Prussia; to the scandalous English aristocrat, Lady Jane Digby, on whom Ludwig may have fathered a child*[29]*; to the exotic dancer known as Lola Montez over whom he lost his throne. By no means all the ladies in the gallery were his mistresses – the most famous portrait is that of Helene Sedelmayr – the daughter of a cobbler whom Ludwig met when she was delivering toys for his children.*

Ludwig lost his head over a flamenco dancer with the stage name of Lola Montez. Lola claimed to be a Spanish aristocrat but was actually an Irish adventurer called Eliza Gilbert. Their affair began in 1846 when Lola got the king's attention (according to different versions of the story) either by pretending to faint in front of him or by baring her bosom[30]*. The sixty-year-old king was infatuated: he wrote that he had thought love was past but his passion for Lola erupted like Vesuvius and he could not eat or sleep*[31]*. Ludwig gave his new love extravagant presents, consulted her on affairs of state, made her a countess (Gräfin Landsfeld), and refused to listen to any criticism. Lola aroused extreme hostility by her boorish and vulgar behaviour – in one incident she poured champagne and chocolates over tipsy students from the balcony of the house in Munich bought for her by Ludwig*[32]*.*

1848 was the year of revolutions across Europe and Munich was already seething. After riots and the resignation of his cabinet, Ludwig came to his senses and banished Lola from Bavaria. But it was too late and in March 1848 he abdicated in favour of his son. Ludwig negotiated a chunky pension and stayed on in Bavaria[33]*.*

Henriette Adelaide called her new schloss *Borgo della Ninfe* or Castle of Nymphs (Nymphenburg). Her building now forms the central pavilion of the schloss where, in the colourful ceiling fresco

of the Stone Hall (Steinerne Saal), nymphs pay tribute to Flora, the goddess of spring, in an idyllic garden landscape. This fabulous, huge room was always the centre of life at Nymphenburg and stretches two stories high across the entire width of the building, with external staircases to allow movement through from the courtyard at the front to the gardens at the back. It is still the centre of things today as visitors have to pass back and forth through the Stone Hall to see the elector's rooms on one side and the electress's on the other. The exuberant rococo decoration of the Stone Hall, in stunning colours of white, gold, and pale green, dates from a make-over by Elector Maximilian III Joseph in the 1750s. I wanted to stay here and gaze for ever, amid the hustle-bustle, and soak up the beauty. The Stone Hall is also a great place for people-watching, chatting to the amicable attendants, admiring brides in their wedding finery, and looking at the gorgeous gardens through the windows.

62. Electress Henriette Adelaide called her schloss the Castle of Nymphs.

When he first came to the throne, Max Emanuel did not take much interest in his mother's schloss. Henriette Adelaide had started to build side wings, which he tore down to use the stone for building Lustheim (see Schleissheim above). But as his ambitions blossomed, Max Emanuel's thoughts turned to Nymphenburg as a summer venue for his court, which by 1701 had mushroomed in size to around two thousand people[34]. In two phases of activity (before and after his years of exile) Max Emanuel built the four side pavilions that define the appearance of Nymphenburg today, in a staggered arrangement of two on each side linked to the original schloss by arcades. He also laid out a magnificent French baroque garden dissected by a water system of canals, ponds, and fountains, as the backdrop for outdoor court entertainments and sports in summer. As well as a hedge (outdoor) theatre, maze, orangeries, and parterres, there were facilities for such aristocratic amusements as *pall mall* (an early form of croquet), bowls, and a sport called *jeu de passe*, which Max Emanuel invented himself and sounds a bit like crazy golf[35]. The French garden was remodelled to an English landscape park in the early nineteenth century, but the bones of the original baroque design were kept, including the canals. These beautiful gardens have been open to the public since 1792 and are a marvellous amenity for the city of Munich.

In 1722, Nymphenburg hosted celebrations to mark the marriage of Max Emanuel's son – the next elector, Karl Albrecht (1697-1745), to Archduchess Maria Amalia of Austria[36]. Karl Albrecht carried on his father's plans for enhancing Nymphenburg, building a semi-circular string of villas, called the Rondell, to form an open courtyard in front of the schloss and developing the gardens. He also created two of the four enchanting mini-schlösser in the gardens, each one fascinating and unique, that are a jewel of Nymphenburg.

Maria Amalia was passionate about hunting and between 1734 and 1739 Karl Albrecht built his wife a small single-storey hunting lodge and called it Amalienburg in her honour. She seems to have been an unusual character for the wife of an eighteenth-century monarch, who had little time for stuffy court etiquette and frequently outraged her ladies-in-waiting by such lapses as allowing her hunting dogs up on the sofa[37]. Amalienburg was designed by the architect François Cuvilliés and is cited everywhere as the most beautiful example of rococo in Germany; one writer even wondered '... whether it is not the most perfect building in the world...'[38]. Maria Amalia put on her special hunting costume and shot pheasants from a little platform on the roof!

63. The rococo Amalienburg has been called
the most perfect building in the world.

The life story of François Cuvilliés provides a fascinating insight
into the eighteenth-century Bavarian court. François was born in
Wallonia (now part of Belgium) in 1695 and when he was eleven,
his physical disabilities (he was short and misshapen) got him a job
with Max Emanuel as court dwarf. The elector was then temporarily
living in Brussels in the early part of his ten-year exile from Bavaria.
A court dwarf was a general factotum and buffoon but Max Emanuel
recognised talent in this one and sent him to Paris to study architecture.
Francois went on to become court architect to Max Emanuel's son,
Karl Albrecht, and one of the most famous names in the history of the
profession.

I love rococo and for me this elegant and playful style works at
its best in smaller, more intimate spaces such as Amalienburg. The
walls of the five rooms along the enfilade are decorated with delicate
carvings and stuccowork gilded in silver (rather than gold) on a
coloured background, alternatively pale blue and golden yellow, room
to room. You can look through the enfilade from one end to the other
and see a dazzling vision of gold and silver, frosted blue, glittering glass

and chandeliers. Quite delicious! The high point is the circular Hall of Mirrors in the centre of the enfilade where the light bounces off tall mirrors and silver birds flutter across the domed ceiling, from silver tree to silver tree. The Amalienburg has quirky touches in keeping with the character of its owner – there is a room for her hunting dogs and a show kitchen where Maria Amalia could do a bit of cooking[39]! The friendly attendant pointed out how the Dutch tiles on the wall in the kitchen must have got mixed up at some point because the patterns don't match, and showed us the imprint of a cat's paw in the tiles on the stove!

On the other side of the gardens to the Amalienburg is another mini-schloss, this one started by his father and finished by Karl Albrecht. In complete contrast to the pleasures of hunting, the Magdalenenklaus is dedicated to death and the transience of earthly life. This weird building is a pretend hermit's retreat with faked-up cracks in the rough brickwork and crumbling plaster to simulate a ruin and the damage caused by the earthquake on judgement day! Inside the Magdalenenklaus is a Grotto Chapel, decorated with artificial coral, shells and coloured stones. Even the spout of water emerging from a vase held by a statue of Mary Magdalene is a fake. Said to be a natural spring of water able to cure diseases of the eyes, it is in fact water diverted from the nearby canal[40]. The Magdalenenklaus also has a monastic suite of rooms where the elector could retreat from affairs of state and pray.

In 1742 Elector Karl Albrecht fulfilled his father's high ambitions when he was elected as the Holy Roman Emperor Karl VII, after the Hapsburg dynasty had run out of male heirs. As the husband of a daughter of Emperor Joseph I, Karl Albrecht reckoned his claim was at least as good as his opponent for the role, who was the husband of Maria Theresa, the daughter of Joseph's younger brother, Emperor Karl VI. In the War of the Austrian Succession Karl Albrecht had his eyes on Austrian territory and made an alliance with France and Prussia.

The Bavarian Swap

After the death of Maximilian III Joseph in 1777, the succession as elector of Bavaria passed to Karl Theodor of Sulzbach (a branch of the Palatine line of the house – see chart 8). Karl Theodor (1724-1799) was not much interested in Bavaria; he was already elector of the Palatine and would have preferred to remain at his schloss in Mannheim. He did however make the final changes at Nymphenburg by adding rooms to the galleries connecting the pavilions; these are today called the Karl Theodor rooms. Karl Theodor had no heir to pass on his great inheritance and was most interested in acquiring ready assets to provide for his illegitimate family. In 1742 he had married Elisabeth Auguste, the granddaughter of his predecessor as elector of the Palatine, but the marriage bombed and after the death of their only son, almost immediately after he was born, the couple lived apart.

So when Emperor Joseph II made diplomatic noises to Karl Theodor about swapping Bavaria for a territory much nearer his Palatine lands called the Austrian Netherlands (now Belgium), he was interested. The idea made huge sense for Austria as it would have given the Hapsburgs a power block in South Germany to consolidate their hold on the Holy Roman Empire and confine Prussia to the North. The plan to make them Austrians did not find favour with the Bavarian people and Karl Theodor was not a popular elector. The Bavarian swap foundered on the stinginess of Joseph II (he never offered enough to tempt Karl Theodor into positive action), the resistance of Bavarians, and the opposition of Prussia and the other Great Powers. The idea finally went away in 1790 when Joseph II died.

Karl Theodor's wife died in 1794 and the seventy-year-old elector quickly made a second marriage to eighteen-year-old Maria Leopoldina of Austria-Este in a last ditch attempt to produce an heir. The marriage was a complete misalliance and another disaster. Maria Leopoldina disliked her husband and would not sleep with him. Instead of trying to produce an heir, she championed the next Wittelsbach branch in line of succession. So Karl Theodor's reign was something of an interregnum and when he died in 1799 he was succeeded by Maximilian IV Joseph of Birkenfeld-Zweibrücken.

But even as Karl Albrecht was being crowned emperor in Frankfurt, the Austrian troops of Maria Theresa invaded Bavaria in pursuit of her husband's claims. Just like Max Emanuel, Karl Albrecht became an exile and only returned to Bavaria shortly before his death in 1745.

The next elector of Bavaria was Karl Albrecht's son, Maximilian III Joseph (1727-1777). He wanted peace at any price. In 1745 Max Joseph signed the Treaty of Füssen relinquishing his claim to the imperial throne or any pretensions for Bavaria as an international power player. In his portrait at Nymphenburg, this elector is depicted not, as his father and grandfather before him, in the pose of a mighty prince and victorious military commander, but relaxing and playing cards surrounded by his extended family. Court life was more restrained and thrifty due to the huge debts he inherited and Maximilian III Joseph became a respected and well-liked monarch of Bavaria. He was very attached to Nymphenburg where he completed the building programme started by his predecessors and

64. The luxuriant Stone Hall was redecorated by Maximilian III Joseph.

redecorated the interior in rococo style (including the Stone Hall). Maximilian III Joseph had no son to succeed him and was the last elector from the Bavarian line of the house of Wittelsbach.

6

BAVARIA AND THE
WITTELSBACH KINGS

The kingdom of Bavaria lasted from 1 January 1806, when Maximilian I Joseph proclaimed himself as king during the Napoleonic Wars, to 7 November 1918 when King Ludwig III secretly fled from Munich following a Bolshevik uprising at the end of World War I. There were six kings in all and they are a distinctly colourful lot. Three were infected with the building bug and one (Ludwig II) took this passion so far it threatened to bankrupt the monarchy and led to him losing his throne. His story is so fascinating that Ludwig II has achieved global superstar status since his death. Four Bavarian kings were deposed or abdicated and only two ended their days still in post. One lost his head over a fake Spanish dancer, two were certified as insane, and the only king of Bavaria to reach his silver jubilee (twenty-five years on the throne) was Otto, who spent his entire reign locked away out of sight. (Please see chart 12 for the kings of Bavaria.)

This chapter includes both some well-known and lesser-known schlösser of the kings of Bavaria. We visit the Versailles look-alike that financially crippled Ludwig II and led to him being deposed, and also the tiny island schloss that was a favourite place in the early years of his reign. We shall see where his brother, Otto, was incarcerated for over thirty years, and also another schloss where a famous royal imposter was unmasked as a fraud.

Casino, Roseninsel

The Casino is a small schloss (a schlösschen in German) on an island in Lake Starnberg called Roseninsel, or Island of Roses. King Maximilian II of Bavaria (1811-1864) bought land on the western lake shore, including the six-acre (two-and-a half hectare) island, from a local fishing family in 1850. He planned to build a summer residence on the shore at Feldafing, but when he died young in 1864 (aged 52) only the Casino had been built, as a garden villa for the private use of the royal family. The island was called Wörth, but was renamed Roseninsel in honour of the rose garden Maximilian planted there.

Lake Starnberg (previously called the Würmsee) in Upper Bavaria was a summer playground for the Wittelsbach family. Further up the shore from Roseninsel is Schloss Possenhofen; the summer home of

65. The small schloss called the Casino on Roseninsel (the Island of Roses); watercolour from 1852.

Maximilian II's distant cousin, Duke Maximilian in Bavaria, who was the father of Empress Elisabeth of Austria (see chart 13). Elisabeth loved the freedom she enjoyed at Lake Starnberg and spent many summers here, even after she was married, staying at Possenhofen or at the Hotel Strauch in Feldafing. On the eastern shore of the lake, opposite Possenhofen, is Schloss Berg. This also belonged to the royal family and was a favourite home of Maximilian II's son, King Ludwig II, in the early years of his reign. Ludwig was found dead in the lake at Berg on the night of 13 June 1886, just days after he was declared insane and deposed as king. A debate still rages over how he, and the psychiatric doctor who died with him, met their ends. Did Ludwig commit suicide, was he accidentally killed trying to escape, or was he murdered?

66. In summer, a small boat takes visitors the short distance to the Roseninsel.

There is no access to Roseninsel by car and we walked down the lake shore, through the park laid out by Maximilian II and past the swimming pool (used by Empress Elisabeth on her visits), to find the small boat that takes visitors the short hop to the island. This is a serene and peaceful spot with distant views of the Alps – the boat glided silently with the swans (it must have an electric motor); the sailing boats and even a passing steamer hardly made a ripple in the water. We were the sole passengers and during the short journey, the boatman gave us his opinion of Ludwig's death. Almost everyone we met in Bavaria seemed to have a view about this. Ludwig is known to have contemplated suicide after he was deposed and faced a life in confinement. But the boatman was adamant that that he would never have done so by drowning because he was such a strong swimmer, who had swum across the lake from Schloss Berg to Roseninsel, a distance of four kilometres. If Ludwig did die by drowning (as is the official cause of death), the view of many in Bavaria is that he must have been injured or even drugged, so that he could not save himself.

How Bavaria became a kingdom

The first king of Bavaria was Maximilian I Joseph (1756-1825). When he was born in 1756, no-one could have predicted such a destiny for him. He was only a younger son from a junior branch of the Wittelsbacher who would have to make his own way in the world. Before the French Revolution he was an officer in the French army. It took the failure to have a son of three higher-ranking Wittelsbach princes, to propel Maximilian Joseph to the top spot. He became Duke of Birkenfeld-Zweibrücken in 1795 on the death of his elder brother; and then Elector Maximilian IV Joseph of Bavaria in 1799 on the death of Karl Theodor (who himself had only succeeded because of the childlessness of Maximilian III Joseph).

Europe was convulsed by the French Revolutionary Wars when Maximilian IV Joseph came into his inheritance. His personal inclinations were towards France and his astute first minister (Graf Montgelas) could see which way the wind was blowing. The elector made an alliance with France and the rewards for Bavaria were considerable, including large increases in territory from the secularisation of the abbeys and church states and a nod from Napoleon, in the December 1805 Treaty of Pressburg, that Bavaria could become a kingdom. On 1 January 1806, heralds rode through the streets of Munich to proclaim King Maximilian I Joseph.

King Maximilian I Joseph was loyal to his French allies and could not be persuaded to desert Napoleon until shortly before his defeat and exile (for the first time) to Elba in 1814. His decision was in time – at the Congress of Vienna at the end of the Napoleonic Wars, Maximilian I Joseph retained his crown and Bavaria kept most of her territory. He was well-respected by his subjects and became popularly known as 'Good Father Max'.

The Casino was built in the two years between 1851 and 1853, and resembles a mixture of Italian villa and Swiss chalet. It is very small – just three rooms on the ground floor, two upstairs, and a third floor viewing room; all connected by a spiral staircase. At the time it was built there was a growing focus on hygiene and indoor plumbing, and an intriguing detail is that both the Queen's Room (downstairs) and the King's Bedroom (first floor) have two en-suite loos. The tour started in the Queen's Room

67. The young Ludwig II on horseback.

where the guide ushered us into one of the loos to take a look out of the window. This was a 'loo with a view' – a wonderful vista of the lake!

The tour was in German with only a scanty one page handout in English; but I was content with looking and enjoying the views. Because I love gardens, I really liked how the rooms have been designed to bring the garden into the house. Downstairs the main room (called the Garden Room) opens out onto terraces on three sides. The main reception room is the Dining Room on the first floor, with windows all round and a large balcony overlooking the rose garden. This stretches down to the lake in a formal pattern of circular paths and beds of roses, with an unusual and striking centrepiece of a blue glass column. This was a gift from King Friedrich Wilhelm IV of Prussia in 1854. Friedrich Wilhelm bought three of the five-and-a half metre tall, bright blue-and-white striped columns and gave the first to his wife Elisabeth, born a princess of Bavaria (she was the aunt of Maximilian II). They had no children, so it is touching to see that the column is topped by a gilded statuette of a little girl feeding grapes to a parrot. The second column went to

Friedrich Wilhelm's sister Charlotte (Tsarina Alexandra Feodorovna of Russia, the wife of Tsar Nicholas I), and the third to his cousin Marie of Prussia (their fathers were brothers), who was the wife of Maximilian II. By the time the state of Bavaria bought Roseninsel in 1970, the glass column had long since disappeared. But parts were discovered in an outbuilding, new pieces were made, and the reconstructed glass column has been back in place in the rose garden since 2001[1].

When Maximilian II died in 1864, his son Ludwig was eighteen years old. Ludwig and his younger brother Otto had rarely been seen in public, so he was virtually unknown. When he appeared in his father's funeral procession in Munich, Ludwig's spectacular good looks made a deep impression on his subjects and the new king instantly gained the great popularity with Bavarians that he has never lost. Ludwig was well over six feet tall, with a slender and athletic figure, blazing blue eyes, and dramatic swept-back, wavy, dark hair. His good looks didn't last and by his thirties, Ludwig was thick-set and heavy. In photographs he wears a heavy overcoat to disguise his corpulent figure[2]. The hairstyle was an affectation; Ludwig's hair was naturally straight and he employed a hairdresser to set it in waves each morning[3].

68. Lake Starnberg showing the Roseninsel and
Schloss Possenhofen on the shore.

Ludwig came to the throne at a bad time, when a tussle between Prussia and Austria for supremacy in Germany would soon lead to war (the Seven Weeks' War of 1866) and he would be forced, reluctantly, to take sides; then see his country's independence truncated as Prussia emerged the victor. He soon found the business of being a monarch was not to his taste and began to retreat into a private world, staying away from Munich as much as possible[4]. Ludwig was often at Schloss Berg. Prince Chlodwig of Hohenlohe-Schillingsfürst, who became his first minister after the Seven Weeks' War, complained that as Bavarian soldiers marched off to war in June 1866, the king was busy setting off fireworks on Roseninsel with Prince Paul Thurn und Taxis (his close companion at that time)[5].

Ludwig loved the solitude and isolation he found on Roseninsel and came to the Casino almost every day when he was at Schloss Berg; rowing across the lake or using his private steamship. Ludwig was an ardent admirer of Wagner and one of his first actions as king was to bring the composer to Bavaria and financially sponsor his work. He called his steamship the *Tristan*, named after the hero in Wagner's opera *Tristan and Isolde*, which premiered in Munich in 1865. My favourite portrait of Ludwig is a water colour by Eric Correns, painted in 1867. This shows him alighting from the *Tristan* after a trip to Roseninsel, carrying a rose in his hand. In the background is Schloss Berg with the tower that Ludwig added to the building and named *Isolde*.

Ludwig planted more roses, extending his fathers' rose garden until there were tens of thousands of roses blooming in the summer and scenting the air. Only a few chosen companions were invited to join him in this fairy-tale retreat. When the actress Lila von Bulyorszky came for dinner at the Casino in 1867 it had been raining, and her evening dress and shoes were ruined on the wet paths in the rose garden. She then feared for her gloves as Ludwig hand-picked some wet roses to give her! Seeing her discomfort, Ludwig promised to replace the roses in another form – Lila hoped for jewellery but received pressed flowers[6].

Lila misunderstood his intentions, because Ludwig was not romantically interested in women and his closest female relationships were with 'safe', older married women. He did become fond of the young Duchess Sophie in Bavaria (daughter of Duke Maximilian in Bavaria), who shared his passion for Wagner, and tried to do what was expected of him by getting engaged to her in 1867. But as the wedding date approached Ludwig panicked, postponed the ceremony several times, and then called the whole thing off. His relief was enormous as shown by this entry in his diary

Sophie written off. The gloomy picture fades. I longed for freedom, thirsted for freedom, to awake from this terrible nightmare[7]!

69. Ludwig II and Duchess Sophie in Bavaria at the time of their engagement.

His fiancé may also have been relieved as her love letters to a young man she met during the engagement photoshoot have since been discovered[8].

Ludwig had an enduring friendship with Sophie's elder sister – *Sisi*, Empress Elisabeth of Austria. In many ways they were kindred spirits, sharing a love of beauty and freedom and a horror of stifling court life and protocol. She called him the *Eagle* and he called her the *Dove*, and they met for platonic trysts at the Casino. Elisabeth often visited Roseninsel when she was staying at Lake Starnberg, even after Ludwig's focus had moved away from the lake to his new castles and mountain hide-outs. She left messages for him to find, such as this poem written by Elisabeth in Amsterdam and left in the Casino on 20 June, 1885.

> Greetings from the North Sea
>
> Eagle up there on the mountains,
> The sea gull sends you
> A greeting of foaming waves
> As far as the eternal snows.
>
> Once we met each other
> Before the grey of eternity
> In the mirror of the loveliest lake,
> When the roses were in bloom[9].

The greatest night in the history of Roseninsel was 26 September 1868, when Ludwig entertained Tsarina Marie Alexandrovna (wife of Tsar Alexander II of Russia) to dinner at the Casino. Ludwig idolized the tsarina, writing her impassioned letters and wishing she was his mother[10]. As night fell, the houses around the lake were illuminated and hundreds of little boats lit by coloured lanterns formed a path for the *Tristan* as she took the royal party back to Schloss Berg. They were accompanied by the lake steamer (called the *Maximilian* after Ludwig's father) with a military band onboard. The grand finale of the evening was a firework display with the tsarina's initials in fire and the sound of the Russian anthem[11].

In later years Ludwig visited the island infrequently but always maintained it in good condition. After his death it was neglected so that the Casino decayed and rough growth covered the rose garden. Restoration began in 1997 and Roseninsel is now open during the summer months (May to October) when there are regular guided tours of the Casino. Schloss Berg remains in the private ownership of the Wittelsbach family and is not open to the public or visible from the road. Visitors can however walk along a path through the schloss grounds to see the cross in the water marking the spot where Ludwig died, and visit his memorial chapel. Schloss Possenhofen has been converted into private apartments and is not publically accessible, but can be seen from the road. There is a museum about Empress Elisabeth in the old railway station of Possenhofen and a six kilometre round tour called the Elisabeth Way taking in the Roseninsel, Feldafing, and Possenhofen.

Linderhof

Linderhof, at Ettal in the Bavarian Alps, is one of three extraordinary castles and palaces built by King Ludwig II of Bavaria (1845-1886). (The other two are Herrenchiemsee (see below) and Neuschwanstein (see Hohenschwangau in chapter 7).) The idea behind Linderhof came from a visit Ludwig made to Paris in 1867 when he was inspired to build his own version of Versailles. Ludwig was a constitutional monarch but he hankered after the absolute style of monarchy epitomised by King Louis XIV of France[12]. Ludwig code-named his building project *Meicost Ettal* which is an anagram of Louis XIV's famous saying

70. Linderhof is like an exquisite carved ivory box – view of the schloss and gardens from the Temple of Venus.

L'état c'est moi (I am the state). The alpine site at Ettal proved unsuitable for the vast scale of Ludwig's new Versailles and this would be built at Herrenchiemsee instead. But the opulent royal villa he built at Ettal pays homage to absolute monarchy and the Bourbon kings of France.

Linderhof is on a compact scale and the exterior is like an exquisite carved ivory box. When we arrived, the building and the hillside behind it were lit up by the early morning sun, as if the schloss was in a spotlight. I would not much like the interior, which I found over-decorated and depressing, but the site and the gardens are just wondrous. A formal baroque garden merges imperceptibly into an English landscape park and then into the beautiful countryside. The best views are from the Temple of Venus, on top of the hillside to the south of the schloss. From here the garden descends in terraces to the water parterre in front of the

71. The fountain in the water parterre sends a jet of water thirty metres in the air.

building; and then up the cascade on the hillside behind it to the Music Pavilion, at the other end of this switchback. Our timing was good – as we stood at the Temple of Venus, the golden fountain in the centre of the water parterre started to play, with a statue of the goddess Flora sending a single jet of water almost thirty metres into the air.

Linderhof is a huge tourist attraction and there are tours in different languages leaving every few minutes. Because the schloss is relatively small, each group has to keep moving at a snappy pace and this was our shortest guided tour, lasting only twenty minutes. It starts in the Vestibule (entrance hall) on the ground floor; dominated by a statue of

Louis XIV on horseback beneath the badge and motto of the Bourbon kings of France on the ceiling. 'Nec pluribus impar' translates formally as 'No-one is my equal' or informally in modern parlance as 'I am the greatest'! Ludwig felt a connection with the Bourbons through his grandfather. He was born on the same day of the year and named after his grandfather, King Ludwig I of Bavaria, who was himself named after, and a godson of, Louis XVI of France (Ludwig is the German for Louis)[13]. Linderhof was the only one of Ludwig's schlösser to be completed and where he regularly lived. The king always carried out a ritual in the Vestibule on arrival – in his memoirs, a servant described how Ludwig embraced the marble pillars and saluted the statue of Louis XIV with a royal gesture[14].

The start of Ludwig's reign in 1864 was full of promise, but unfortunately a series of early disappointments encouraged him to turn his back on public life and retreat into a fantasy word he created from his own imagination[15]. From boyhood, Ludwig was solitary and dreamy. A teacher once found him sitting alone, staring into space. But when it was suggested he have something read aloud, so as not to be bored, Ludwig replied that he was not bored at all – his imagination kept him amused[16]!

The new king's first building projects were at the Residence Schloss in Munich. He also planned a new opera house for Munich to stage Richard Wagner's operas. But after Wagner was forced to leave Bavaria against Ludwig's will in 1865, and the plans for the opera house were shelved, he turned his back on the capital city. There would be no more projects in Munich or plans for great public buildings. A passion for building would devour Ludwig's life and his fortune, and ultimately lead to his downfall as king. But from now on his energies were focused on his private retreats and in creating a parallel world where he could pretend to live in a past that he found more sympathetic. At Linderhof, Ludwig was driven around the countryside at night in a golden rococo sleigh, with coachmen, lackeys, and out-riders dressed in period costume[17]. He lived alone but food was prepared, and the dining table

Schlittenfahrt Sr. Majestät des Königs Pudwig II.

72. Ludwig II was driven around the countryside at night in a sleigh,
with servants in period costume.

set for three or four, so he could entertain and converse with imaginary
guests from the long-gone court of France – Louis XIV, Louis XV,
Madam Maintenon or Madame Pompadour[18].

Ludwig's projects were strongly influenced by his love of opera and
theatre and around the park at Linderhof he built pavilions and follies
(also now open to the public) where he could act out different roles.
The rustic Hunding's Hut is based on the first act of Wagner's opera
Die Walküre and conjures up a world of Germanic legends; here Ludwig
reclined on a bear-skin rug and drank mead from a drinking horn. The
Venus Grotto is a man-made hillside cavern where Ludwig recreated
the lascivious *Venusberg* from the first act of Wagner's *Tannhäuser* and
was rowed across an indoor artificial lake in a shell-shaped boat. Flick
a lighting switch and it became the Blue Grotto at Capri. The Venus
Grotto was the largest artificial cave in the world and used technology
to achieve effects such as a rainbow and waves on the lake.

One of the pleasures of writing about schlösser is discovering new
sources and books I have not read before. For this book, they include
the memoirs of Theodor Hierneis, who was a cook in the kitchens of

Ludwig II and one of the servants with him on his last day of life at Schloss Berg[19]. When he joined the royal staff as a fourteen-year-old kitchen-boy on 1 November 1882, the first question Hierneis was asked was whether he had enjoyed a good sleep the night before, since he could expect to get none that night. By this stage of his life Ludwig had so lost touch with reality that he reversed day and night; getting up in the evening and going to bed in the morning. This meant that all his meals were served during the night and his kitchen-boy suffered the agonies of a growing teenager, struggling to stay awake in the kitchens. Hierneis' account of Ludwig's strange rules for staff documents how far the king's eccentricities had gone – servants were not allowed to look at him, must stand bent double in his presence, and apologise in writing for any misdemeanours. The footman, Meyer, had to wear a black mask because Ludwig did not like his face. Yet Hierneis wrote of Ludwig in affectionate terms and says his behaviour was accepted because he was the king.

From the Vestibule the tour goes through the ten rooms that make up the first floor of the schloss and were used by Ludwig (the ground floor was for servants). Although Linderhof was a private home, their names echo the great state rooms at Versailles – the King's Bedroom, Audience Room, and Hall of Mirrors. The rooms are small and the elaborate rococo decoration is quite overpowering with almost every inch of wall space embellished by extravagant gilding, paintings, hangings, and mirrors (you can get an idea from illustration 73). Ludwig was very involved in the detail of his projects and instructed that more decoration and more gilding be added. In his fascinating biography, Greg King says Ludwig's eyesight got worse as he grew older and he was too vain to wear glasses; so the décor in his castles became more and more excessive[20]. The blinds were drawn during our tour, to keep out the sun, and the dim lighting added to the general feeling of gloom. I couldn't imagine living here without getting depressed, and had to remind myself that Ludwig's waking hours were at night when everything would have looked very different in the candlelight!

But the artistry and craftsmanship needed to produce these interiors is astonishing and I admired the work without liking the finished effect. Ludwig's commissions kept the workshops and studios of Munich busy, as well as those of Paris and Vienna. In the King's Bedroom, the walls are hung with the most amazing panels of goldwork hand-embroidery, worked on blue velvet. I know from my own experience that these must have taken dozens of embroiderers many years to complete. I also liked the two large porcelain peacocks in luminescent colours that stand in the Tapestry Rooms. These would be placed on either side of the entrance when Ludwig was expected at Linderhof.

73. The East Tapestry Room houses one of the porcelain peacocks that were placed at the entrance when King Ludwig II was expected.

Ludwig moved frequently between his castles, hunting lodges (he inherited eighteen of these from his father), and mountain retreats. He usually travelled at night and sometimes stayed in one place only for a night or two. His kitchen staff travelled with him and, in his memoirs, Hierneis vividly describes the problems of trundling over the night-time countryside with a mule wagon carrying their equipment and supplies. The cooks had to arrive ahead of the king and serve him the same high standard of food, whether at the Munich Residence or in a borrowed forester's hut in the hills[21].

I was surprised to learn that Linderhof was not built from scratch but evolved in stages (between 1869 and 1878) from an old wooden hunting lodge owned by Ludwig's father and where he had often come as a child. Ludwig first added extra rooms and then new wings to the lodge until, in 1874, he had the original building dismantled and re-erected a short distance away. Called the Royal Lodge, it is still there and houses a very good exhibition about the building of Linderhof. Everything is in German but the curator lent us an extensive handout that translated all the material. The Royal Lodge was ignored by most other visitors when we were there, not helped by a silly ticketing system that required an extra entrance fee at the door. On an easel outside was a delightful portrait on glass of Ludwig's favourite horse, foraging from his al-fresco breakfast table at the Royal Lodge[22].

Schloss Tegernsee and the Dukes in Bavaria

When Maximilian IV Joseph of Birkenfeld-Zweibrücken became the elector of Bavaria in 1799, the only other surviving branch of the house was the Birkenfeld-Gelnhausen branch, headed by his second cousin, once removed, Duke Wilhelm (1752-1837) (see chart 13). Maximilian IV Joseph gave his

cousin a new title and created Wilhelm the first Duke in Bavaria in 1799. It is important now to distinguish the slight difference in title between the Dukes of Bavaria (from the senior, Birkenfeld-Zweibrücken, branch) and the Dukes in Bavaria (from the junior *Birkenfeld-Gelnhausen branch.)* Maximilian IV Joseph became King Maximilian I Joseph of Bavaria on 1 January 1806.

Schloss Tegernsee was originally a Benedictine Abbey, established in the eighth century. The abbey was secularised in 1803 and King Maximilian I Joseph bought the buildings in 1817 and converted them into a royal residence. Several plaques in the porch of the Abbey Church commemorate royal events that took place at Tegernsee, including a meeting of the king with the emperors of Austria and Russia in 1822 and the marriage of his daughter Ludovika.

In September 1828, Princess Ludovika of Bavaria (1808-1892), married Duke Maximilian (Max) in Bavaria (1808-1888) the grandson of the first duke in Bavaria; Tegernsee then became a home of the Dukes in Bavaria. Max (see illustration) and Ludovika had ten children who included Empress Elisabeth of Austria, Princess Helene of Thurn und Taxis (see St Emmeram in chapter 4) and Duchess Sophie (who almost married Ludwig II). Their brother Duke Karl Theodor in Bavaria (1839-1909) became a professional oculist (most unusual for a prince then) and founded the Duke Karl Theodor Eye Clinic in Munich.

The Birkenfeld-Gelnhausen branch of the house of Wittelsbach died out with Duke Ludwig Wilhelm (1884-1968), who was the son of Karl Theodor. But the line of Dukes in Bavaria continues because Ludwig Wilhelm had adopted Max Emanuel (born 1937) as his heir to the title. Max Emanuel, Duke in Bavaria, is the younger brother of Franz, Duke of Bavaria – who is the current head of house Wittelsbach. Tegernsee remains a Wittelsbacher home and also houses the famous Duke of Bavaria brewery and beer house and the Tegernsee Grammar School.

Herrenchiemsee

Herrenchiemsee was built by King Ludwig II of Bavaria on an island in Lake Chiemsee. For hundreds of years this island, called Herreninsel (Men's Island), was home to a monastery and the nearby (smaller) island, called Fraueninsel (Women's Island), to a convent. After the monastery was dissolved in 1803, the island passed through the hands of a series of private owners until it was bought by a wood-processing company around 1871. There were public protests when the company began chopping down the trees and Ludwig bought the island in 1873 to save it from deforestation[23]. Since his first visit to Paris a few years before, the king had been drawing up plans to build a Bavarian Versailles and the island was the site he had been searching for[24]. Construction work on the new palace began in 1878.

74. Herrenchiemsee was Ludwig II's version of Versailles
– the garden front and Latona fountain.

The only way to get to Herrenchiemsee is by scheduled boat service from the town of Prien am Chiemsee on the western shore of the lake. Around half a million visitors come to the schloss each year, but we arrived early and the nine am departure was almost empty. The schloss is in the centre of the island, completely surrounded by trees, and it was a twenty minute walk from the pier before we emerged out of the trees at the far end of the garden. Ludwig planned to lay out extensive formal gardens around Herrenchiemsee, similar to those at Versailles. But at the time of his death in 1886, only the central axis of the garden was complete, cutting an alley east/west through the centre of the island. From where we stood, the view to the east was up through the formal garden to the garden façade of the schloss. Behind us, looking west, the Grand Canal led out into the lake.

Herrenchiemsee is not an exact copy of Versailles; rather it is Ludwig's own version and interpretation. The building work was not completed when he died, but he never intended the schloss to be fully finished in the normal sense. He part-built two long side wings to flank the main block, as at Versailles, but the inside of these were to be left as builder's shells. These side wings were demolished in 1907. And in the surviving central section of the schloss, Ludwig only ever marked eighteen of the seventy odd rooms to be fitted out[25]. Not all of these were finished and, at the end of the guided tour, we left through another builder's shell – what was intended to be a grand staircase but still has brick walls, plain wooden ceiling, and concrete steps.

The gardens are a gracious blend of flower-beds, gravel paths, water basins, and fountains. When Ludwig made a second visit to Paris in 1874 (the year after he purchased Herreninsel), he celebrated his twenty-ninth birthday at Versailles and the fountains in the gardens were turned on especially for him. (It caused grumbling in the French press about the cost to a country still impoverished from losing the Franco-Prussian War.[26])

And right on cue, the fountains at Herrenchiemsee were turned on, as if for us. The Latona Fountain is a copy of the fountain of the same name at Versailles and depicts the goddess Latona surrounded by peasants she has turned into frogs for refusing to give her water when she was thirsty. I found these grotesque figures unsettling, with their human bodies, frogs' heads, and agonised, gaping, mouths. But happily when the water started to play, the grotesque half-humans of my mind's eye were transformed into frolicking half-frogs.

The guided tour goes through the State Apartments in the south and west wings, which correspond to the ceremonial rooms at Versailles. In some respects, Ludwig's version is better than the original, and this includes the grand entrance called the Ambassadors Staircase, where the tour began. It no longer existed at Versailles when Ludwig went there (it was demolished in 1752) and had to be recreated at Herrenchiemsee from old engravings. Although he was building in the style of the past, Ludwig incorporated the latest technology and building techniques. The glass roof over the Staircase would not have been technically possible in the original and is a stroke of genius, flooding this gorgeous space with light. The contrasting colours of the two floors of the staircase are symbolic, and represent day and night. On the first floor the colours glow with orange and gold and the statue of Apollo (the sun god) is a reference to Louis XIV (*the Sun King*). In contrast, the ground floor is cool in blue and grey and the goddess of the night, Diana, could stand for Ludwig as he was a night person who slept during the day[27].

75. The Hall of Mirrors at Herrenchiemsee surpasses that at Versailles.

The State Apartments at Herrenchiemsee are bigger and more opulent than their models at Versailles, where much had been lost because of the French Revolution, and the rooms were empty even when Ludwig visited. If such a thing is possible, the decoration is even more extravagant than at Linderhof (see above), so that I could hardly believe it was real. I felt as if I was walking through a stage set or an imaginary painting. But whereas at Linderhof the overall effect is oppressive, here, in the larger spaces at Herrenchiemsee, it is magnificent!

The Hall of Mirrors stretches the length of the garden front (west wing) and, at nearly one hundred metres, is considerably longer than at Versailles (by seven and a half metres). The tall windows all the way down one side of the room are reflected in a row of mirrors on the opposite wall. Ludwig recreated decoration that had been lost in this room at Versailles and the result is breath-taking. Rows of giant, floor-standing, gold and crystal candelabra line the room on each long side; above them hang lines of gold and crystal chandeliers. Together the forty-four candelabra and thirty-three chandeliers hold two thousand two hundred candles. When Ludwig stayed in the schloss, they were all lit and would have been endlessly reflected in the glass and mirrors. Until 1982 concerts in the Hall of Mirrors were still held by candlelight; but then health and safety regulations intervened[28]!

A corridor from the Hall of Mirrors leads to a second set of rooms called the Small Apartment. These room were for Ludwig's personal use but are also extravagantly furnished and decorated. Ludwig stayed in this apartment only once – for just nine days between 7 and 16 September 1885 – on what would be his last visit to Herrenchiemsee[29]. He had been to the island several times before, to review building progress, but always stayed in rooms converted for him in the old monastery. On this last visit, Ludwig was disillusioned when he rapped a statue with his cane and it shattered into pieces. Unbeknownst to him, because of the shortage of money, plaster had been substituted for marble[30]!

Wildenwart and Queen Mary III of Great Britain

Just ten minutes away from Lake Chiemsee by car, Schloss Wildenwart at Frasdorf is still in the private ownership of the Wittelsbach family. It came

into the Bavarian royal house when Queen Maria-Theresa, the wife of King Ludwig III (1845-1921), inherited it from her uncle, in 1875. He had bought the dilapidated schloss from a mining company a few years before and restored it.

Maria-Theresa is better known to supporters of the Stuart or Jacobite claim as Queen Mary IV of Scotland and Queen Mary III of Great Britain and Ireland. She was a direct line descendant of Henrietta Anne, the youngest sister of King Charles II. Henrietta's descendants had a better claim than the Hanoverians, by order of birth, to succeed Queen Anne, but were overlooked because they were Catholic.

Ludwig III and Maria-Theresa were the last king and queen of Bavaria. They were forced to flee Munich secretly on the night of 7 November 1918 following a Bolshevik take-over. Maria-Theresa was already ill with cancer and had to be lifted into the car. As a diversionary tactic Ludwig let slip that their destination was Schloss Leustetten near Lake Starnberg (also still owned privately by the Wittelsbacher) but they arrived at Wildenwart in the early hours of the following morning after an eventful journey. Later that same day they fled further – over the frontier into Austria. The king refused to abdicate, but on 13 November he released the army and civil servants from their oath of allegiance.

When things quietened down, the ex-king and queen returned to Wildenwart and Maria-Theresa died there on 3 February 1919. Neither her son, Crown Prince Rupprecht (King Robert I), nor his successors as head of house, have actively pursued the Jacobite claim to the throne of Britain.

Financially, Herrenchiemsee was a schloss too far for Ludwig. He spent more than 16.5 million marks on the building work, twice as much as at Linderhof and nearly three times as at Neuschwanstein[31]. The building costs spiralled out of control and still the Bavarian Versailles was far from finished! By the end of 1885, Ludwig's debts had reached a staggering fourteen million marks against his annual income from the civil list/appanage of three point four million[32]. The king was caught in the throes of an obsession; he could not stop building and was working on plans for even more new castles. He was desperate for money – seeking loans in the most unlikely places and cooking up a hare-brained scheme to rob banks[33]! It has been said that Ludwig used his own money to fund his projects (rather than public money). But I think this is a fudge because much of his income came from the state as the civil list, and this money was intended to support the functions of the monarchy rather than fund private spending. At the end of the day, the government would be expected to stand behind the king's debts. Ludwig was seeking further government funds and wrote to his mother that 'Through some kind of manipulations it must be possible for the cabinet to bring matters back on track'; she was of the view that the state of Bavaria should pay off his debts[34].

76. The king was caught in the throes of an obsession for building.

With the connivance of his uncle Prince Luitpold (his father's younger brother), the Bavarian cabinet of ministers began plotting to depose Ludwig on the grounds he was mentally unstable and unfit to rule. For years he had been a most unsatisfactory king, neglecting his duties and refusing to appear in public. And now unsavoury rumours were circulating; not just about Ludwig's debts, but also about his homosexual liaisons with soldiers and stable-boys, his reclusive and nocturnal lifestyle, and his alleged abuse of servants. On 9 June 1886, a panel of four eminent psychiatrists, including Dr Bernhard von Gudden, declared Ludwig to be insane (suffering from paranoia) on the basis of evidence collected. This came mainly from ex-servants and government spies – incredibly, the doctors never examined Ludwig personally. On 10 June, Prince-regent Luitpold was declared to be the new ruler of Bavaria.

Ludwig was detained at Neuschwanstein on 12 June and taken in a locked carriage to Schloss Berg on Lake Starnberg, where he was to be interned. He was forty years old. The schloss had already been modified

for use as a lunatic asylum with spy holes drilled in the doors, door handles removed from the inside of rooms, and bars put on the windows. The ex-king's behaviour had normalised since his detention and this seems to have lulled Dr Gudden into a false sense of security. So when on the following day, 13 June, Ludwig requested an evening walk in

77. Ludwig II lying in state – a debate still rages over how he died.

the grounds, the doctor agreed. There are indications that, on this last day, the ex-king was planning to escape. As the two men left the schloss just after six pm, Ludwig was seen to unbutton his overcoat and jacket even though it was a wet and stormy evening. Was this for a quick get-a-way? As they took the path towards the lake, Dr Gudden made a fatal mistake when he waved back the two medical attendants who were following them. This meant there were no witnesses to what happened next and no help forthcoming when the doctor lost his life in some kind of struggle. When the two did not return, a search was instigated and, late that night, the bodies of King Ludwig II and Dr Bernhard von Gudden were pulled out of the lake.

What exactly happened will probably never be known unless and until the house of Wittelsbach releases the papers in their Secret Archive (the name for the private family archive). Did Ludwig commit suicide or accidentally drown while trying to escape (perhaps by suffering a heart attack)? Did he kill the doctor when he tried to prevent him? Or (far less likely), was it all a conspiracy and Ludwig was murdered by the Bavarian government to whom he had become an embarrassment? On his death, the government took over Ludwig's schlösser and by August Herrenchiemsee was open to the fee-paying public. How Ludwig would have hated that!

Fürstenried

A plaque in the gardens commemorates the one-hundred-year anniversary of the death at Fürstenried of King Otto of Bavaria. He died on 11 October 1916, in the middle of World War I. Otto is a sad figure and I think of him as the forgotten king of Bavaria because his name is often left out of the list of sovereigns – the name of his uncle, Prince-regent Luitpold, is substituted instead. Otto became king in 1886 following the violent death of his brother, King Ludwig II (see Herrenchiemsee above), but he was already suffering from mental illness and his reign was subject to a regency. He was on the throne for twenty-seven years, although Otto was king only in name and confined throughout at Fürstenried as his private and exclusive lunatic asylum. Prince-regent Luitpold, who was the next heir to the throne, carried out the functions of the monarch and was king in all but name. Luitpold had participated in the coup to depose Ludwig II and, because of this, very wisely never tried to dethrone Otto and take his place. But after the prince-regent died, his son took advantage of a change in the constitution to depose Otto in 1913 and become King Ludwig III.

78. Fürstenried was the home of the mentally ill King Otto of Bavaria
from 1883 until his death in 1916.

For the last three years of his life, he was ex-King Otto. (Please see chart 12 which lists the kings of Bavaria).

The plaque in the garden was put up by the Archdiocese of Munich and Freising, who have owned Fürstenried since 1925 and use it as a Catholic Retreat House. The schloss is not open to the public but we were very kindly invited to see inside. The exterior of the schloss and the layout of the buildings and garden still look very much as they do in an eighteenth-century hunting print and a garden plan from King Otto's time, both hanging on the walls inside[35]. A modern flat-roof building on one side of the garden (built in the 1970s) is well camouflaged with trees. But the interior of the schloss has long since been altered and modernised to suit its new use, and very little of the historical décor remains. I do not have a problem with this because finding a new purpose is why Fürstenried has survived the last century in such good condition. Only in the Jagdzimmer (Hunting Room) on the second floor is some of the original cornice still in place.

Fürstenried was built by Elector Maximilian II Emanuel between 1715 and 1717 as a hunting lodge. It was part of his complex of palaces around Munich that he planned to link up by canal and incorporate into great sweeping vistas (the others were Schleissheim, Nymphenburg and Dachau). When it was built Fürstenried was out in the countryside, but the city of Munich has long since overtaken it and the schloss is now in the suburbs, close to a busy dual-carriageway road. Inside the schloss it is surprisingly quiet and peaceful, very much in keeping with a retreat and place for contemplation, prayer, and spiritual renewal. The garden is a green haven cut off from the outside world by a wall and we drifted past elaborate stone statues, pergolas of trained lime trees, and avenues of hornbeam, informal copses, and the Waldcapelle (Forest Chapel). In the 1940s Fürstenried was a temporary home for the theology faculty of the Ludwig-Maximilian University of Munich and the young Joseph Ratzinger studied here for the priesthood. Later he would become Cardinal of Munich and Freising and, in 2005, Pope Benedict XVI. He wrote

The years at Fürstenried abide in my memory as a time of great change, filled with hope and promise, as well as a time of critical and anguishing decision. When I occasionally visit the Park, which remains unchanged, the external and internal paths I had walked are so intertwined that I stand afresh before all my memories[36].

In 1727, Fürstenried was a gift from Elector Karl Albrecht to his wife Maria Amalia to mark the birth of their first son – the future Elector Maximilian III Joseph (chart 11). The schloss then became a dower house and was the home of Maria Amalia in widowhood and later of her daughter-in-law, Electress Maria Anna Sophia, who lived at Fürstenried from the death of Maximilian III Joseph in 1777 until her own death twenty years later. During these years Maria Anna Sophia became a very popular figure because of her campaign to keep Bavaria independent and thwart the plan to hand over the country to Austria (see *The Bavarian Swap* in Nymphenburg, chapter 5). The widowed

79. The foyer of the schloss, which is now a Catholic Retreat House.

electress pushed the rights of the next heirs from the Birkenfeld-Zweibrücken branch (as pensioners of France they were unlikely to support a scheme that favoured Austria) and held meetings, wrote manifestoes, and kept up a correspondence to lobby Frederick the Great of Prussia[37]. The Bavarian swap never materialised and Maria Anna Sophia played a role in its defeat by speaking up and generally making herself a nuisance.

After the electress's death, Fürstenried was used in a variety of ways (including as a barracks and military hospital) before it was converted to provide a residence for King Otto. As a young man, Otto (born in 1848) had been cheerful and gregarious and often undertook public engagements on behalf of his reclusive elder brother, Ludwig II. Otto followed the usual military career for German princes and took part in two wars – the Seven Weeks War of 1866 and the Franco-Prussian war of 1870. But his war experience damaged his mental equilibrium and he began to show signs of serious disturbance. In 1871 his brother wrote in a private letter

It is really painful to see Otto in such a suffering state which seems to become worse and worse daily ... He often does not go to bed for forty-eight hours; he did not take off his boots for eight weeks, behaves like a madman, makes terrible faces, barks like a dog, and, at times, says the most indecorous things; and then again he is quite normal for a while[38].

Ludwig decided that Otto would never be sent to a psychiatric hospital but would be kept out of the public eye and looked after privately. He lived first at Nymphenburg before being moved, as his behaviour deteriorated, to the more secure Fürstenried in 1883.

80. Queen Marie of Bavaria with her sons Ludwig and Otto; both would be deposed as king.

Photos of Otto after his confinement are rare and in those I have seen he is restrained (or supported?) by two attendants holding his arms[39]. He lived in some comfort but Fürstenried was essentially a prison. The schloss was guarded by soldiers and Otto was only allowed into the garden under supervision[40]. He was treated by Dr Bernhard von Gudden who would later be brought in to diagnose his brother and who died with Ludwig II in the waters of Lake Starnberg.

Dr Gudden was a respected practitioner and an advocate of humane treatment for mentally ill patients with no use of physical restraint; but Otto was probably sedated with drugs. A medical report of June 1886 mentions his 'mental disturbance, pronounced states of exaltation, depression, hallucinations, compulsive movements, and delusions'[41]. It is hard to be sure but perhaps his disease was schizophrenia which can develop in young people in their twenties. Otto's mother, Queen Marie, always visited her son, but after she died in 1889 he was isolated and there were few who would remember the merry Otto of his childhood. Ex-king Otto died of appendicitis on 11 October 1916, aged sixty-eight [42].

Kloster Seeon

I wanted to come to Seeon to see the grave of Anastasia Manahan. Mrs Manahan died in Charlottesville, Virginia, on 12 February 1984 but asked to be laid to rest at Seeon, near the grave of Duke Georg of Leuchtenberg, who had died long before, in 1929. Members of the Leuchtenberg family did not want her in their family cemetery but the Local Authority intervened and Mrs Manahan's ashes were interred in the churchyard of St Walburg church at Seeon in June 1984. During her life she was known by several names, including Anna Anderson, Anastasia Tchaikovsky, and Fräulein Unknown (Unbekannt). Her supporters believed she was the Grand Duchess Anastasia Nikolaevna, the youngest of the four daughters of Tsar Nicholas II of Russia, and that she had been miraculously saved when the entire family was massacred at Ekaterinburg on 17 July 1918. Duke Georg gave her shelter in his home at Seeon and when a witness from her real past turned up at the schloss to unmask her, he let the moment pass. The false Anastasia went on to maintain the pretence for the rest of her life and her identity was only confirmed in 1994 (ten years after her death) when DNA testing showed her to be a Polish factory worker called Franziska Schanzkowsky – just as the witness had said all those years before.

81. Seeon is a converted monastery on an island in the Klostersee.

Schloss Seeon (usually called Kloster Seeon) came into the ownership of the Leuchtenberg family when it was purchased in 1852 by the Dowager Empress Amalie of Brazil. She was a daughter of the founders of the Leuchtenberg dynasty – Eugene de Beauharnais and Auguste Amalie of Bavaria (please see chart 7 for a Leuchtenberg family tree). The schloss was a converted Benedictine monastery on a small island in the Klostersee (Monastery Lake) not far from Herrenchiemsee. After the monastery was dissolved in 1803 as part of secularisation, the property was sold off to a private owner (a Munich baker) and the island was joined up to the shore by a causeway in 1816.

When Amalie bought it, Seeon was being run as a spa hotel with a bathing hall in the old monks' refectory where guests wallowed in heated tubs of the island's spring water, rich in sulphur, to treat gout, arthritis or rheumatism[43]. She appointed a manager and expanded the spa but it was never really a paying proposition. When she died, Amalie left Seeon to her sister, Queen Josephine of Sweden, and she sold it on to their nephew, Duke Nikolai Maximilianovitch of Leuchtenberg. The duke died in 1891 and Seeon came to his younger son, Georg.

The Leuchtenberg family

The Leuchtenbergs were an important dynasty that was closely connected to several royal thrones. The first duke of Leuchtenberg was Eugene de Beauharnais (1781-1824), the son of Empress Josephine of France by her first marriage (she married Napoleon as a widow). Napoleon strong-armed a dynastic marriage for his step-son and in 1806 Eugene married Princess Auguste Amalie, the daughter of King Maximilian I Joseph of Bavaria. Father and daughter were given little choice (it was a condition of Bavaria becoming a kingdom) but Eugene was essentially a nice man and the marriage was happy. They had six surviving children, three of whom married ruling sovereigns.

After the Napoleonic Wars, Eugene was awarded money by the Congress of Vienna and he used this to purchase the Bavarian estate of Eichstätt from his father-in-law. King Maximilian I Joseph also created him duke of Leuchtenberg.

Eugene died at the early age of forty-two and was succeeded by each of his two sons in turn. The elder married Queen Maria da Gloria of Portugal in 1835 but died from illness just two months after the wedding, aged twenty-four. In 1839 the younger son, called Maximilian, married Grand Duchess Maria Nikolaevna, daughter of Tsar Nicholas I, and made his home in Russia. The Leuchtenberg men often did not have long lives and he died in 1852, aged thirty-five.

The fourth duke, Nikolai Maximilianovitch, was a great favourite with the Russian royal family. But he fell out with his mother (Grand Duchess Maria) and his uncle (Tsar Alexander II) over his morganatic marriage to a divorced commoner. The couple were forced to leave Russia and their two sons were born abroad – Nikolai in 1868 and Georg (who sheltered Anastasia at Seeon) in 1872. The family lived mostly at Schloss Stein an der Traun in Bavaria, just a few miles from Seeon. The boys had the title of duke (herzog) but no dynastic rights, because of the status of their parents' marriage. When Nikolai Maximilianovitch died in 1891 (aged forty-seven) the position of head of house passed to his next brother, Eugene.

KLOSTER SEEON
Sketch Map

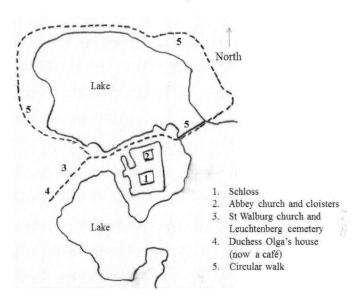

↑ North

Lake

Lake

1. Schloss
2. Abbey church and cloisters
3. St Walburg church and Leuchtenberg cemetery
4. Duchess Olga's house (now a café)
5. Circular walk

After Georg left the Russian army in 1905, he and his family relocated from Russia to live in Kloster Seeon. He was an accomplished author and in his memoirs written late in life (called *Reflections of the Past*) Georg describes with great affection the wonderful times they all had at Seeon[44]. The family returned to Russia on the outbreak of World War I where Georg re-joined the army. They had considerable difficulty getting out again after the Revolution and the abdication of the tsar, and Georg's youngest son, sixteen-year-old Andrei, died of typhus with the White Army in 1919. An entry in the guest book at Seeon for 27 September 1920 says simply 'At last we are back'[45]. Georg considered it his duty to help other Russians and the schloss became a sort of boarding house for assorted exiles. Anastasia Tchaikovsky (as she was then called) arrived at Seeon as his guest in February 1927. Georg was related to the real Anastasia (his grandmother and her great-grandfather were brother and sister) but had not known her in person.

Seven years before, on 27 February 1920, a disturbed young woman had been pulled out of a canal in Berlin. She had no papers, refused to give her name, and spent the next two years in a mental hospital registered as 'Fräulein Unknown'. After a while another patient said she recognised her as a daughter of the tsar. The claim that she was

Grand Duchess Anastasia would split the Russian émigré community into opposing camps, confuse the identity experts on both sides of the argument, be the subject of lengthy court cases, and provide material for numerous articles and books for the next seventy years. And yet her real identity was there to see almost from the start.

In early April 1927 (soon after she arrived at Seeon) a Berlin newspaper published articles under the headline 'The Unmasking of the False Grand Duchess Anastasia'. They produced evidence to show she was in fact Franziska Schanzkowsky,

82. Duke Georg and members of the Leuchtenberg family are buried in St Walburg church at Seeon.

who had been reported missing by her Berlin landlady soon after the attempted suicide of the unknown woman in a Berlin canal. Duke Georg believed the evidence, writing to a relative that 'the documents shown to him seemed to leave no doubt'[46]. With his consent, it was agreed that the landlady's daughter, Doris Wingender, would be brought to Seeon to unmask the fraud. The meeting took place in Anastasia's room on the second floor of the schloss and she chose to face it out, burying her head under the blankets and staying silent. When her brother, Felix Schanzkowsky, was produced a month later, she persuaded him to keep quiet and leave her to her new life. This was a policy that the entire Schanzkowsky family, who well knew who she was, followed until after she was dead. So the moment passed, allowing Anastasia's camp to argue that Doris had been paid by the newspaper to tell lies, and that Felix had not said she was his sister. Duke Georg said

I can't tell you if she is the daughter of the tsar or not. But so long as I have the feeling that a person who belongs to the tight circle of my society needs my help, I have a duty to give it[47].

Anastasia/ Franziska left Kloster Seeon in January 1928; Duke Georg died there the following year. Money was running short in the Leuchtenberg family and in 1934 the schloss was sold at auction. Georg's widow, Duchess Olga, stayed on in a small house next to St Walburg church and when she died in 1953, a hundred years of the Leuchtenberg family at Seeon came to an end.

Today Kloster Seeon is a cultural centre and conference hotel owned by the regional government of Upper Bavaria. The monastery church and cloisters are open to visitors and there is a small café and shop. The schloss is connected to the village of Seeon on the far side of the lake by a narrow wooden walkway and there are nice views from a circular walk taking around thirty minutes. Page 155 has a hand-drawn sketch map showing the layout. I came hoping to see the Leuchtenberg family cemetery in St Waldburg church (next door to Kloster Seeon) and both the churchyard and church were open. Here lies Duke Georg, in an elaborate Russian Orthodox memorial, surrounded by members of his family. The grave of Mrs Anastasia Manahan is on the edge of this family group. The date of birth on her headstone is not correct – Grand Duchess Anastasia was born in 1901, but Franziska was five years older.

83. Memorial to the false Anastasia.

Berchtesgaden

Schloss Berchtesgaden is my favourite schloss in this book. Most overseas visitors come to Berchtesgaden to see the site of Hitler's holiday home on the Obersalzberg, and to visit the mountain-top teahouse called *the Eagle's Nest* that the Nazi party gave him as a fiftieth birthday present. So I was thrilled to discover a traditional Alpine village and a schloss with a history that goes back nine hundred years. Berchtesgaden was a favourite with the Bavarian royal family long before Hitler came to power and the personality that has stamped itself most on this schloss is that of Crown Prince Rupprecht of Bavaria (1869-1955) – an opponent of the Nazis who spent the war years in exile and whose wife and children were sent to concentration camps.

84. Schloss Berchtesgaden is captivating – (left to right) the Abbey Church, Provost's Wing and the Crown Prince's Wing.

The village of Berchtesgaden is set in a valley surrounded by a ring of mountains. There are glimpses of the schloss from a distance, but it is not until you walk through the arch into the courtyard (Schlossplatz or Palace Square) that you get a view of the front, with the Abbey church on the left, Provost's wing in the centre, and the Crown Prince's wing (named after Rupprecht) on the right. This is not a grand or austere palace, but a captivating and friendly building decorated in pink and white like the icing on a cake. I could see straightaway why members of the Wittelsbach family liked to spend time here in the summer months and still do today.

85. Crown Prince Rupprecht with his second wife, Antonia, and their five eldest children.

The schloss developed from an old Augustinian monastery founded by Graf Berengar of Sulzbach in 1102 to honour a pledge made by his mother. When her husband went missing during a hunt, Gräfin Irmgard had vowed to establish a religious house if he was found safe again (he was). In the fourteenth century the monastery and surrounding land became a sovereign church state in the Holy Roman Empire called the Provosty of Berchtesgaden (the head monk was called the provost). This state was so small it was joked that the Provosty was 'as high as it was broad'[48]. But Berchtesgaden had a strategic location (close to the present-day border with Austria), wedged between the duchy of Bavaria and the Archbishopric of Salzburg, and was also very rich because of its salt mines (*white gold*). In 1559 the provost was raised to the rank of prince and over the next centuries the medieval monastery was turned into a prince's palace. The prestigious position of prince-provost was held by some of the highest ranking families, including (from 1715) by a son of Elector Maximilian II Emanuel[49]. The monastery was dissolved in 1803 and a few years later (1810) the old Provosty of Berchtesgaden became part of Bavaria and the schloss passed to the house of Wittelsbach.

The first Wittelsbach to stay here was King Ludwig I, who became so fond of Berchtesgaden that he kept the right to use the schloss even

after his abdication in 1848. So the next king, Maximilian II, had to build a second schloss in the village for his own use. The Royal Villa was built between 1849 and 1852 in Florentine style. Like father, like son – Ludwig I, his son Maximilian II, and his son Ludwig II, were all three passionate builders. The young Ludwig II came to Berchtesgaden with his parents

86. The Royal Villa was built by King Maximilian II.

often as a child. We saw where Ludwig's height at six years old was marked on a doorframe when they visited his grandfather in the old schloss. The Royal Villa is now a restaurant and private apartments and in front of it is Luitpold Park, named after Prince-regent Luitpold who liked to come to Berchtesgaden during the hunting season. Luitpold and his son, King Ludwig III, were avid hunters and are often depicted in their photographs and portraits wearing hunting gear. A statue of the prince-regent in his hunting shorts stands in Luitpold Park.

Berchtesgaden was the home of Crown Prince Rupprecht and his second family between 1922 and 1933 (for his first marriage, please see New Residence Bamberg in chapter 2). Rupprecht was the son of Ludwig III and head of house after his father's death in 1921. That same year, fifty-one-year-old Rupprecht married twenty-one-year-old Princess Antonia of Luxembourg. The couple had first become engaged at the end of World War I but were forced to wait because of the unpopularity of Germans in Luxembourg[50]. Rupprecht and Antonia had six children (a boy and five girls) between 1922 and 1935. Their eldest daughter, Irmingard, who was born in Berchtesgaden in 1923, wrote a biography about growing up in the schloss, and other Wittelsbacher residences, and what happened to the family in World War II[51]. The guided tour includes the children's rooms in the Deanery wing and the long corridor where, as Irmingard recalls, they played on rainy days.

87. The Gothic Hall houses fifteenth-century works of art.

The original contents of the monastery were dispersed when it was dissolved and everything in the schloss now was brought from other Wittelsbacher schlösser. The family were great collectors and Rupprecht showed exquisite taste in selecting and arranging the contents. This is what makes Berchtesgaden so very special. The schloss developed over centuries in different architectural styles, starting with romanesque in the twelfth-century cloisters and then finishing with the rococo salons from the 1780s. The crown prince followed the approach of matching the contents of each room to its age and style, and the result is stunning!

The Gothic Hall, where the tour begins, was built around 1400 and houses sacred works of art from the fifteenth century. Rupprecht dedicated the mid-sixteenth-century renaissance rooms to Duke Ottheinrich of Palatine-Neuburg (1502-1559) and decorated them with three magnificent portals (doorways) that the duke commissioned for Schloss Neuburg (see chapter five) between 1538 and 1558. Ottheinrich's portrait hangs in these rooms. The rococo salons are in elegant Louis XVI style with delicate stucco work and mirrors. These are the venue each September for the *Berchtesgaden Talks* when Duke Franz invites prominent politicians and scientists to discuss current affairs.

The guided tour also shows the twelve rooms on the first floor of the south wing furnished by Rupprecht in 1922 as his private apartment. Princess Antonia's rooms (not shown) were on the floor

88. The Grand Dining Room in Rupprecht's private apartment.

above and their children's in the Deanery wing. The Crown Prince's Suite includes his study, where a half-finished jigsaw puzzle was on his desk (Rupprecht enjoyed doing jigsaws); the Men's Room where they were allowed to smoke and which still whiffs of cigars; and the Grand (for parties) and Small (for everyday use) Dining Rooms. The main schloss kitchen is some distance away and was last used for cooking in 1955, when Rupprecht's youngest daughter, Sophie, got married. Duke Franz and the family still use these rooms on visits to Berchtesgaden for the Salzburg Music Festival and behind a disguised door in the Small Dining Room is a modern kitchen.

Crown Prince Rupprecht was popular in Bavaria and during the years he lived at Berchtesgaden there was a widespread belief that he would soon be recalled as king. His father had never officially renounced his claim to the throne so that after Ludwig III died in 1921, Rupprecht considered himself to be the lawful heir. In his book on the history of the kings of Bavaria, first published in 1933, Henry Channon wrote that '...without the Wittelsbachs there is something missing;' and '... there is a growing feeling among all classes that the time has come for them to resume power.'[52]. But instead the Nazis gained ground. After Hitler became chancellor of Germany in 1933, it was no longer sensible for Rupprecht and his family to stay in Berchtesgaden. They moved to Schloss Leustetten near Lake Starnberg until this was confiscated in 1939 on the outbreak of war.

The crown prince was a passive opponent of Nazism and he spent the war years in exile in Italy. After the failure of the plot to assassinate Hitler on 20 July 1944 (see Greifenstein in chapter 2), Rupprecht was forced into hiding; Antonia and her five daughters (aged nine to twenty-one) were arrested and sent to concentration camps. They survived to be liberated and paintings and drawings by Irmingard after the war document their experiences and the sufferings of concentration camp prisoners[53]. Antonia was so traumatised and broken in health (she weighed only five and a half stone when released) that she never returned to Germany and died in a Swiss clinic on 31 July 1954 from the after-effects of her mistreatment[54]. Rupprecht still hoped to regain his father's throne but this was never in the mind of the Allied occupying forces. He devoted his last years to his art collection and died on 2 August 1955.

At the end of the guided tour, a door from the children's corridor on the second floor opens onto a small garden. The Upper Rose Garden has a sixteenth-century fountain, hundreds of pink rosebushes, and spectacular all-around views of alpine meadows and mountain peaks. From here you can see up to the tea-house on the top of Kehlstein mountain which the American Army christened *the Eagle's Nest*. Schloss Berchtesgaden has everything to enchant the visitor – beautiful setting, exquisite contents, an interesting history of its own, and the enthralling story of Crown Prince Rupprecht. We even got the guided tour in English, courtesy of the only other two (German) visitors! This is how I met a fellow royal history enthusiast and made a new friend.

The house of Wittelsbach today

The current head of the house of Wittelsbach is Duke Franz of Bavaria, born in 1933. The courtesy title of Duke of Bavaria was first used by his father. It is afforded as a courtesy to the head of house and is not an official rank or title. Since the end of the German monarchy in 1918, former nobility is no longer recognised and former royal titles can only be used as part of a surname. All members of the main (Birkenfeld-Zweibrücken) branch of the house, including Duke Franz, have the surname Prince (or Princess) of Bavaria (Prinz/Prinzessin von Bayern). Members of the subsidiary (Birkenfeld-Gelnhausen) branch use the surname Duke (or Duchess) in Bavaria (Herzog/Herzogin in Bayern). (Please see chart 8 for the branches of the house).

Duke Franz has never married and the heir presumptive as head of house is his younger brother Max Emanuel, born in 1937. Since 1968 Max Emanuel has also been Duke in Bavaria, following his adoption as an adult by the last of the Birkenfeld-Gelnhausen branch (see Tegernsee above). So, should he survive his elder brother, Max Emanuel would be in the interesting situation of being both Duke of Bavaria and Duke in Bavaria.

Succession to the head of house Wittelsbach follows the principle of Salic law and excludes females. I understand there are no current plans to change this. Max Emanuel has five daughters and the next male dynast in the family is his second cousin Luitpold Prince of Bavaria, born in 1951. Luitpold's grandfather was a younger brother of Crown Prince Rupprecht; Luitpold's mother was Princess Irmingard of Bavaria, the eldest surviving daughter of Crown Prince Rupprecht (she married her first cousin). It sounds complicated but please see chart 14 for the family tree of the house today and the succession as head of house. The Salic law applies only to the dynastic position as head of house and not to the inheritance of property.

89. Statue of Prince-regent Luitpold in Berchtesgaden, wearing hunting clothes.

Luitpold Prince of Bavaria has three sons born in the 1980s. The eldest, Ludwig Prince of Bavaria (born 1982), works with Duke Franz to learn about the management of the family funds. Ludwig is also the founder of an innovative initiative in rural Kenya, called Startup Lions, providing opportunities and jobs for youngsters in the IT sector. Heinrich (born 1986), the middle son, married Ms Henriette Gruse in April 2017.

After Luitpold's male descendants, the next male dynast in the house (with male issue) is his first cousin Wolfgang, born in 1960. Wolfgang has three sons, born in the 1990s. With so many males in the next generation, the future of the house seems secure.

Duke Franz inherited the Stuart or Jacobite claim to the throne of Great Britain (see Wildenwart above). The Salic law does not apply here and the next in line after his brother is Sophie, born in 1967 (Max Emanuel's eldest daughter). Sophie is married to Prince Alois, the heir to the throne of Liechtenstein; they have three sons and a daughter.

7

SWABIA,
THE PRINCE-BISHOPS
OF AUGSBURG AND
THE WITTELSBACH KINGS

The area called Swabia in the south-west of Germany is split across the federal states of Bavaria and Baden-Württemberg. In the middle-ages, Swabia was a mighty duchy ruled by the Hohenstaufen dynasty of Holy Roman emperors. But after the Hohenstaufen line died out in 1268 the duchy declined and splintered into pieces until there were scores of different territories in Swabia; the most important of these were the Duchy of Württemberg, the Margraviate of Baden, and the Bishopric of Augsburg. When the Holy Roman Empire was dissolved during the Napoleonic Wars, Württemberg became a kingdom and Baden a grand duchy (these are now in the federal state of Baden-Württemberg). The Bishopric of Augsburg was secularised and became part of the Kingdom of Bavaria.

Our last schlösser are in the south of Bavarian Swabia, in the foothills of the Alps, close to the border with Austria. We see the schloss that inspired King Ludwig II to build his dream castle at Neuschwanstein and another that is not what it seems at first sight. And we hike uphill to see the main attraction at a twenty-first century theme park about castles.

Hohenschwangau

One day in spring 1829, when he was on a walking tour near Füssen in Swabia, seventeen-year-old Crown Prince Maximilian (1811-1864) came across the old ruined castle of Hohenschwangau. Maximilian fell in love with the romantic setting and the crumbling buildings and decided that he wanted to buy the schloss. The prince was the heir to the Bavarian throne and was looking for a bolthole from his rigid life in Munich under the strict supervision of his father, King Ludwig I[1]. He later wrote that discipline and firmness were the main criteria for his upbringing and that 'Toughening me up was exaggerated to the point where I suffered from frostbites on both my hands and feet.'[2]

90. Hohenschwangau was the perfect holiday home of King Maximilian II and Queen Marie.

Maximilian asked his art teacher, the architectural artist and theatre designer Domenico Quaglio, to arrange the purchase and undertake the restoration. But it took a long time to do the deal because the vendor could sense that the prince was keen and held out for a high price. Eventually, in 1832, Maximilian bought Hohenschwangau for 7,000 guilders. Over the next five years the old ruin was transformed into one of the most enchanting places I have ever been. This delightful mock-medieval castle, with ochre-coloured walls, blue and white striped blinds, and a magical interior where the walls are painted with history, is set in a jewel of a garden amid stunning mountain scenery, and must have been the perfect holiday home.

91. Crown Prince Maximilian.

Hohenschwangau translates literally as the High Swan Country and the history of the schloss goes back to the Knights of Schwangau who were the lords of this area in the medieval period. Schwan means swan and legend has it that the ancestor of these lords (a knight called Driant) appeared one day on the Alpsee (the lake below Hohenschwangau) in a boat drawn by a swan. Maximilian imported swans from abroad (both white and black swans) and there is a romantic portrait of him, painted by Lorenzo Quaglio (brother of Domenico) in 1841, sitting in a rowing boat on the Alpsee feeding the birds, with Hohenschwangau in the background. Over the centuries the schloss passed through the hands of many owners and by the end of the Napoleonic Wars it was in ruins and ripe for demolition.

Domenico Quaglio designed the new Hohenschwangau in neo-gothic style and it is the perfect example of a nineteenth-century version of a medieval castle. He supervised every detail of the rebuilding and refurbishment down to the garden ornaments and the selection of soft furnishings. The furniture was made to his instructions and he chose the colour of the upholstery material for the chairs to match the paintings. Quaglio was a stickler for detail and for quality even though he could hardly sleep at night for worrying about the mounting costs. Originally estimated at around 12,000 guiders, these had already risen to over 100,000 by 1835[3]. Quaglio's high standards are one reason why the schloss is so charming – everything fits together and feels harmonious. Hohenschwangau was Domenico Quaglio's swan-song – the architect-artist had a stroke and died there in 1837.

92. The Lion Fountain in the gardens was designed by Domenico Quaglio.

From early on, Maximilian decided to have the rooms at Hohenschwangau decorated with scenes from German and Bavarian history. These colourful and fascinating murals are a unique feature of the schloss and a huge part of its charm. Each room has a specific theme which is explained in gothic lettering painted on the wall over the door. Right from the start the schloss was open for tourists when the royal family was not in residence, and these labels were there to help visitors understand the paintings. The prince was influenced by his history teacher, Josef von Hormayr, in a belief that history has the propaganda power to influence current-day thinking[4].

In the Schyren Room the murals show legendary deeds of Maximilian's ancestors (Schyren was the family name of the forbearers of the Wittelsbacher). Here is Otto I (the first duke of Bavaria) protecting the Holy Roman emperor during a battle in 1155, and his son, Ludwig I, proposing to Ludmilla von Bogen in 1204. Their marriage brought the Bogen blue and white lozenges into the Wittelsbach coat-of-arms. In the Hall of the Knight of the Swan (the dining room) the paintings tell the legendary saga of Lohengrin, the Swan Knight. The murals were painted directly on the wall, surrounded by a painted frame, which has led to problems of conservation from damp and cracking plaster ever since Maximilian's day.

In 1842, after a trawl of the available princesses, Maximilian (now thirty) married sixteen-year-old Princess Marie of Prussia, a cousin of King Friedrich Wilhelm IV. Like her husband, Marie fell in love with Hohenschwangau at first sight and she later described it as 'my favourite place on earth'[5]. The couple had two sons – Ludwig (later King Ludwig II) born in 1845 and Otto (later King Otto) in 1848 – and the whole family spent several weeks at Hohenschwangau each year. Marie's rooms are on the first floor and Maximilian's on the second, with a concealed staircase connecting their separate bedrooms. When he became king in 1848, the schloss was no longer big enough to accommodate his suite, and in 1854 Maximilian II built the Prince's building. When the boys were older, they had their rooms there.

Marie enjoyed taking exercise and she loved the mountains. While her husband was out hunting, Queen Marie became a pioneer of the sport of female hiking (a very unusual hobby for a woman at that time). She climbed most of the mountains in the vicinity and designed her own mountaineering outfit to make the going easier (see illustration 93) with leggings under a calf-length skirt and crinoline, traditional tall hat, and a stout stick. She also established the *Order of the Alpenrose* and awarded this to courtiers who could keep up with her[6]! The boys were often out hiking with their mother and Ludwig II got his great love of the mountains from those childhood holidays at Hohenschwangau.

93. Queen Marie wearing the special mountaineering costume she designed.

You only have to stand in Maximilian's bedroom to understand the effect Hohenschwangau had on his eldest son's imagination; here is the inspiration for Ludwig II's dream castles. The walls are painted all the way around with sensual scenes from a renaissance poem by Torquata Tasso about a crusading knight called Rinaldo. He is put under a spell by the naked enchantress Armida and carried off to her magic garden in a golden chariot pulled by dragons[7]. In 1855, Maximilian had the naked figures overpainted with clothes, probably to protect the innocence of his sons; these were removed on a restoration in 1961. The bedroom ceiling is painted as the night sky with the winged figure of a naked woman representing sleep. After Maximilian's death, Ludwig II took over his father's rooms and had pinholes cut in the sky so that lights could be placed in the room above to shine through as stars.

Neuschwanstein

When he became king in 1864, Ludwig II loved Hohenschwangau more than any of his other homes, but felt it was tainted by the continued presence of his mother, Queen Marie. So he decided to build his own version of a medieval castle on the next door peak. The foundation stone for Neuschwanstein was laid in 1868 and for the next sixteen years Ludwig watched it go up through a telescope from his window at Hohenschwangau. Ludwig's rooms at Neuschwanstein were only ready for occupation in 1884.

Although he was recreating a world based on the past, Ludwig was a firm believer in modern technology, and incorporated many innovations at Neuschwanstein, such as structural steel beams, automatic flushing toilets, a telephone, and the latest in kitchen equipment. But the schloss was never finished and Ludwig only ever saw Neuschwanstein as a building site.

Ludwig was detained by a state commission at Neuschwanstein on 12 June 1886. He had been advised to take pre-emptive action, either by fleeing the country or by returning to Munich to appeal to his people; but he seemed to be apathetic and let fate take its course. When he asked for the key to the tower, there were fears he would try suicide by jumping off the top. Ludwig was transferred to Schloss Berg, where he died the following day (see Herrenchiemsee).

Neuschwanstein rises above the still blue waters of the Schwansee (Swan Lake) against the spectacular scenery of the Bavarian Alps. Built by the Dream King of Bavaria as an escape from dreary reality, it touches the public imagination as the perfect vision of a fairy-tale castle. The towers and turrets of Neuschwanstein were an inspiration for the Disney castle and nearly one and a half million visitors come here each year to see the dream.

King Maximilian II suffered from ill-health and died in 1864 at the relatively young age of fifty-two. During the tour our guide told us that the king died from blood-poisoning following a fall from his horse. When I asked for clarification the guide then announced that although this was the official story, the real cause of death was syphilis contracted as a young man during a foreign trip in 1833 (I have seen both these causes mentioned in different sources[8]). In 1833 Crown Prince Maximillian made a three-month trip to Greece and Turkey and this is commemorated in the Oriental Room (Queen Marie's bedroom) which is furnished and decorated in Oriental style. The ceiling is painted with Moorish arches and the murals commemorate the places Maximilian visited, including the highlight of an audience with Sultan Mahmud II in the Beylerbey palace in Constantinople (Istanbul).

Maximilian II suffers from the misfortune of being sandwiched in history between the flamboyant personality of his father (Ludwig I was forced to abdicate amid the furore over his affair with a flamenco dancer – see Nymphenburg) and the near-legendary status of his son (*Mad King Ludwig II* or *The Dream King* – see Linderhof and Herrenchiemsee).

94. Aerial view of Hohenschwangau in the foothills of the Alps.

There has been very little written about Maximilian in English and he is portrayed as a dull intellectual (his epithet in history is *The Professor on the throne*) whose poor parenting may have contributed to the personality disorders of his sons. Maximilian's public image reminds me of his contemporary Prince Albert (1819-1861), the husband of Queen Victoria, who also made a mess of bringing up his eldest son and has come down in history as worthy but dull. Queen Marie has had a bad press from historians too, as a loving but distant mother who brought mental instability into the family and was not bright enough to share her husband's interests. You only have to go Hohenschwangau to understand that these are one-dimensional pen-pictures. I really hope there will be a biography of King Maximilian II in English soon.

Queen Marie died at Hohenschwangau in 1889 and the schloss then became a favourite haunt of her brother-in-law, Prince-regent Luitpold, who loved to go there for the hunting. Luitpold, who became acting monarch on the overthrow of Ludwig II in 1886 (see chart 12), refused to use the king or queen's rooms and instead occupied an apartment on the third floor where he made modern improvements such as installing electricity and a lift. From a shaky start, the prince-regent became a popular and respected figure in Bavaria and a symbol of stability. A feature of Hohenschwangau is the display of many valuable 'Prince-regent gifts' that Luitpold received from grateful subjects on his big decade birthdays (seventieth, eightieth, and ninetieth).

The guided tour of Hohenschwangau takes thirty-five minutes and goes through Maximilian and Marie's rooms. The furniture is original and visitors see these rooms much as they were designed by Quaglio. I have to admire the good organisation that allows so many people to walk through and enjoy this schloss. Tours were starting every five minutes from the courtyard, in different languages, with a large electronic scoreboard displaying tour information and controlling visitor entry. We were on the English tour starting at 9.50am and as soon as our number came up on the scoreboard the automated barriers accepted our tickets and let us through. Impressive!

What happened to the Wittelsbach schlösser
when the monarchy was abolished?

Because of the rapid expansion of territory and absorption of other principalities when Bavaria became a kingdom, the house of Wittelsbach had an extraordinary number of schlösser. After the monarchy was abolished in November 1918, the question arose as to what should happen to the property of the ex-ruling dynasty. The republican government of the new Free State of Bavaria initially intended to expropriate their assets, but there was a good legal argument that the house should be compensated. The impact of the arrangements of 1818 had also to be considered, whereby King Maximilian I Joseph had ceded the dynastic assets of the house in return for an annual appenage (similar to the arrangement made by George III of Great Britain in 1760 and known as the Civil List). With the end of the monarchy this arrangement became null and void and there was an argument that the assets reverted to the Wittelsbacher.

Following lengthy negotiations, an agreement was reached between the government and the house in 1923 that resulted in a three-way solution. Under this agreement, most of the schlösser were ceded to the state, but others remained in the ownership of the house, and some were contributed, together with art treasures, to a new organisation called the Wittelsbacher Ausgleichsfonds (WAF) or Wittelsbach Compensation Fund. The WAF, which still exists today, is a foundation set up by act of parliament with the purpose of ensuring that Wittelsbach schlösser and art treasures are accessible to the public, with the income paid over to the Wittelsbach family. I have not come across this unique solution for any of the other ex-reigning families.

The Wittelsbach schlösser in this book owned by the state of Bavaria include Trausnitz, Burghausen, Schleissheim, Nymphenburg, Herrenchiemsee, and Linderhof. Berchtesgaden and Hohenschwangau are owned by the WAF. Wildenwart, Leustetten, and Tegernsee Abbey remain in the private ownership of the Wittelsbach family.

Hohes Schloss Füssen

The Hohes Schloss (High Castle) at Füssen is only five kilometres from Hohenschwangau, but was a complete contrast to the busy crowds we experienced there. Walking up the hill (called the Schlossberg) towards the entrance, on a path cut from solid rock by Prince-bishop Friedrich II at the end of the fifteenth century, the only other visitors we saw were a couple pushing bicycles. The entrance to Hohes Schloss is theatrical as the path narrows, turns back on itself, and then enters the courtyard by a dark tunnel through the Gate Tower. And here the curtain rises on an unexpected surprise – the facades of all three wings are covered with unique paintings dating from 1499. Visitors do a double-take as what at first sight looks like a myriad of architectural features (including turrets, gables, oriel windows, and decorative stonework) turns out to be an illusion. These are trompe l'oeil, or illusion paintings, and the trademark of the schloss.

95. The Hohes Schloss at Füssen was the summer residence of the prince-bishops of Augsburg.

The Hohes Schloss was the summer residence of the prince-bishops of Augsburg, the rulers of an independent church state in the Holy Roman Empire called the Bishopric of Augsburg. After the Bishopric became part of Bavaria, the Hohes Schloss was considered as a possible summer residence for Crown Prince Maximilian. But repeated damage in different wars over the centuries meant that, when it was inspected by a building commission in 1832, the schloss was rejected as structurally unsound[9]. But the rejection did have the positive effect of focusing attention on the Hohes Schloss and efforts were made to repair it and find a commercial use. The district court and prison took over two of the three wings (the south and west wings) in 1862, and these remain in government use today as offices for the tax authority. The main (north) wing, which includes the historic rooms of the prince-bishops, was restored in the first part of the twentieth century and opened as a museum in 1931, showing paintings from the Bavarian State Art Gallery. The highlight of this museum is undoubtedly the Rittersaal (Knights' Hall) with a magnificent carved wooden ceiling dating from 1500 and incorporating portraits of patron saints of the Bishopric of Augsburg – St Afra, St Simpert and St Ulrich.

96. The Rittersaal (Knights' Hall) with carved wooden ceiling from 1500.

The beginnings of a schloss at Füssen go back to the Romans and a small fort on the top of the Schlossberg, there to guard the Roman military road called the *Via Claudia Augusta*. This important route ran north/south from the Danube to Venice through a pass in the Alps, and was used by armies, travellers, and traders for centuries. Füssen was strategically located on the route, just north of the Alps on the bank of the River Lech, and the prosperity of the town was founded on the old Roman road. Over time, the fort fell into ruins but in 1291, Duke Ludwig III of Bavaria (known as the Severe) began illegally building a new schloss on the site. It was all part of a tussle about sovereignty over the Benedictine monastery of St Mang. This monastery was founded on the Schlossberg in the ninth century on the site of the death-place of a peripatetic monk and miracle worker called St Mang (or Magnus)[10]. The problems over the monastery began when Duke Konradin of Swabia died without an heir in 1268. Konradin (1252-1268) was the last of the Hohenstaufen noble family who provided several Holy Roman emperors (see Trausnitz in chapter 5). He bequeathed St Mang to his uncle, Ludwig III, but unfortunately this contravened an earlier treaty and led to confrontation with the two other princes with an interest in this area – the prince-bishop of Augsburg and Graf Meinhard II of the Tyrol (who was Konradin's stepfather). The emperor (Rudolph I reigned 1273-1291) tried to calm things down by taking over the monastery himself and declaring Füssen an imperial free city. But as soon as he died the conflict broke out again and Ludwig III started illegally to build his schloss. Quite understandably, the abbot of the monastery did not relish sharing the Schlossberg with a fortified castle, but it took complaints and threats from the prince-bishop to get Ludwig to back off.

The prince-bishop eventually got his hands on St Mang in 1313, when the incumbent emperor was unable to pay his debts. The monastery had been mortgaged to the Bishopric as security for loans to finance the emperor's military campaigns. When the mortgage could not be redeemed, the monastery and town became part of the Bishopric and Füssen ceased to be an imperial free city[11]. In 1322, Prince-bishop Friedrich I bought the Schlossberg from the abbot and then finished

97. The unique illusion paintings are the trademark of the schloss.

building the Hohes Schloss as a secondary residence. The schloss and the monastery have shared the skyline of the Schlossberg ever since.

The second prince-bishop to have a key impact on the Hohes Schloss was Friedrich II von Zollern (reigned 1486-1505). The large painting of Christ as Saviour of the World (Salvator Mundi), which opens the State Art Gallery in the prince-bishops' rooms, was donated to the schloss by Friedrich II in 1494. He remodelled the old castle into a prince's palace and was responsible for the illusion paintings on the outside and for the ceiling in the Rittersaal. From this high point the gradual decline of the Hohes Schloss began, until it was held to be structurally unsound by the building commission in 1832. Restoration work has continued on a stop/go basis until the present day, as and when funds were available. Those marvellous (and unique) illusion paintings were restored between 1956 and 1998.

98. The Hohes Schloss in the 1830s when it was assessed as a possible summer residence for Crown Prince Maximilian.

The Hohes Schloss was a nice place to end our tour of Bavarian schlösser. From the sixth floor of the Gate Tower there is a beautiful panorama of the town of Füssen and surrounding countryside. The dead-straight road heading north is a reminder of the old Roman road called the *Via Claudia Augusta*, where the history of the schloss began.

World of Castles Ehrenberg and Highline 179

Over the centuries, schlösser have survived through war, fire, neglect, and the fall of the German monarchy. I am amazed at how these wonderful buildings have continually adapted with the times and reinvented themselves to find commercial uses in the twenty-first century. World of Castles Ehrenberg is a great example.

Füssen is close to the Bavarian border and our route took us on a loop through the Austrian Tyrol. Suddenly, there was a narrow glass bridge hanging high above the road. Highline 179 is a four-hundred-metre-long walkway, one metre wide, suspended one hundred and fifteen metres above the B179 at Reutte, just over the border in Austria. The Highline stretches between two ruined hill-top castles – Schloss Ehrenberg (built by Graf Meinhard II of the Tyrol in 1296) on one side of the valley; and Fort Claudia (built in 1639 by Archduchess Claudia de Medici, who was regent of the Tyrol) on the other. You can buy a ticket to walk the bridge from one schloss to the other but this is not for the faint-hearted or anyone who does not like heights!

The defences of these schlösser were disabled in 1782 and they have been in ruins ever since. But the site is now a castle theme park called

Burgenwelt (World of Castles) Ehrenberg, with Highline 179 as the main attraction. A new museum called 'On a Knight's Trail' takes visitors on a journey with a fourteenth-century knight as he sets out to make his fortune; and hiking paths lead up to the Highline. We hiked up to Schloss Ehrenberg to see it, but were not brave enough to venture out onto the bridge.

8

FAVOURITE SCHLÖSSER

Bavaria is a beautiful part of Germany, with its own unique culture and history, and a real joy to visit. The state was once a kaleidoscope of different sovereign territories so that, from Franconia in the north to the Alps in the south, the Bavarian countryside just teems with fascinating castles and palaces built by these dukes, princes, and bishops. Some aspects of Bavarian royal history are quite well known (such as the enthralling story of *Mad King Ludwig* and his fairy-tale castles), but other parts were a wonderful surprise. By visiting their schlösser I discovered for the first time the fabulously rich Thurn und Taxis at Regensburg; the talented Schönborn who had such a big influence on Franconia; a tiny state in the Alps called Berchtesgaden that grew rich on salt; and much, much, more ... I hope this book will encourage you to get off the beaten track and go and see these wonderful places for yourself.

With so many beautiful schlösser in Bavaria to choose from, it was hard to decide which to include in this book and which to leave out, or to restrict the contents to twenty-five (the format for my *Schloss* books). This is why there are ten additional schlösser featured more briefly in the text boxes. For each schloss, I have tried to give a brief account of some of the colourful history; and also a flavour of the experience of an overseas visitor. In my view what makes for the best visits is a combination of beautiful surroundings, intriguing history, and (above everything else) a welcoming staff. From among the twenty-five schlösser in this book, I have some favourites and these are listed below. They cover a range of ages, architectural styles, families, and size of visitor numbers. Some of the visits I enjoyed the most were at the least-well-known schlösser that rarely see an English-speaking visitor. But the common denominator of all these favourite schlösser is that they were great fun to visit.

The author's favourite schlösser in this book

Berchtesgaden – *a captivating schloss in a converted old monastery in a stunning alpine location; this became the home of Crown Prince Rupprecht and is where he arranged treasures from the Wittelsbach art collection in an exquisite setting.*

Hohenschwangau – *the picturesque holiday home of King Maximilian II and Queen Marie of Bavaria, who both loved the mountains; this is where well-organised tours allow hordes of visitors to enjoy their visits.*

Nymphenburg – *an elegant summer palace with a gorgeous garden built to celebrate the birth of an heir to Bavaria; a favourite with the Wittelsbach electors and with the people of Munich today.*

Greifenstein – *a delightful mix of museum and family home in Franconian Switzerland, owned by the Stauffenberg family for over three hundred years, with a passionate guide who made our visit memorable.*

Weissenstein – *the baroque masterpiece and private retreat of Lothar Franz von Schönborn – the prince who said he was infected by a 'building worm'.*

99. The last king and queen of Bavaria –
King Ludwig III and Queen Maria-Theresa.

My overall favourite is Berchtesgaden and this joins the top picks from my three other books on the *Fascinating Royal History of German Castles* – Ludwigslust in Mecklenburg-Western Pomerania in the first book (*Schloss*), Bückeburg in Lower Saxony in the second (*Schloss II*), and Augustusburg in North Rhine-Westphalia in the third (*Schloss II*). In all of these, as at Berchtesgaden, the staff went the extra mile to give us a great visit.

The book began at Bamberg in Franconia, in a schloss on the tourist route called *The Castle Road* (www.burgenstrasse.de). It ends at Hohes Schloss Füssen, at the southern end of another famous route called *The Romantic Road* (www.romanticroadgermany.com). This winds its way for four hundred and ten kilometres north to south, past schlösser in Bavaria and Baden-Württemberg. I can't wait to return and see more of these for my next book (the fifth) on schlösser in Baden-Württemberg.

100. The baroque schloss at Rastatt in Baden-Württemberg
will be in my next book.

I want to thank everyone who helped with this book including Gert-Juergen Frisch for invaluable information on the Wittelsbacher and Martin Modes for contacts in Coburg. Ian Callaway did a great job on the design of both the cover and interior. Thank you also to all the museum curators and attendants who welcomed us and patiently tried to answer my questions and search out material in English, particularly the Wittelsbacher Ausgleichsfonds (WAF). I strongly recommend a visit to their wonderful Museum of the Bavarian Kings in Hohenschwangau village. But most of all I thank my husband, Terry, for providing the photographs and charts which are such an important part of the books, and also helping in so many other ways – chauffeuring me around Bavaria, acting as a sounding board, and reading and re-reading the text.

APPENDICES

The map opposite (which is hand drawn) shows the regions of the federal state of Bavaria in Germany and the approximate location of the twenty-five schlösser included in this book. Please use the list below to match the numbers with the individual schlösser.

1. New Residence Bamberg
2. Seehof
3. Weissenstein
4. Greifenstein
5. Kaiserburg Nuremberg
6. Ansbach
7. Ehrenburg
8. Veste Coburg
9. Callenberg
10. St Emmeram
11. Burgruine Donaustauf
12. Trausnitz
13. Burghausen
14. Burg Tittmoning
15. Neuburg
16. Schleissheim
17. Nymphenburg
18. Casino, Roseninsel
19. Linderhof
20. Herrenchiemsee
21. Fürstenried
22. Kloster Seeon
23. Berchtesgaden
24. Hohenschwangau
25. Hohes Schloss Füssen

APPENDIX A
MAP OF BAVARIA

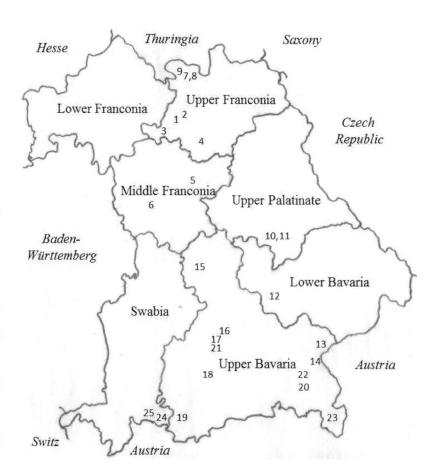

APPENDIX B
LIST OF THE SCHLÖSSER INCLUDED IN MY BOOKS

Name (location if different)	Family	Current use	Book
Bavaria			
Ansbach	Brandenburg-Ansbach	Government offices & Museum	IV
Bamberg New Residence	Prince-bishops Bamberg	Museum	IV
Berchtesgaden	Wittelsbach	Museum & Private	IV
Berg	Wittelsbach	Private	IV
Burghausen	Wittelsbach	Museum	IV
Callenberg (Coburg)	Saxe-Coburg-Gotha	Museum & Private	IV
Donastauf	Thurn und Taxis	Museum	IV
Ehrenburg (Coburg)	Saxe-Coburg-Gotha	Museum	IV
Forchheim	Prince-bishops Bamberg	Cultural centre & Museum	IV
Fürstenreid (Munich)	Wittelsbach	Religious retreat	IV
Füssen	Prince-bishops Augsburg	Museum	IV
Greifenstein (Heiligenstadt)	Stauffenberg	Private with Museum	IV
Herrenchiemsee	Wittelsbach	Museum	IV
Hohenschwangau	Wittelsbach	Museum	IV
Ketschendorf (Coburg)	Saxe-Coburg-Gotha	Under renovation	IV
Landshut Residence	Wittelsbach	Museum	IV
Laufen	Prince-bishops Salzburg	Commercial offices	IV
Linderhof (Ettal)	Wittelsbach	Museum	IV
Neuburg	Wittelsbach	Museum	IV
Neuschwanstein (Hohenschwangau)	Wittelsbach	Museum	IV
Nuremberg	Holy Roman emperors	Museum	IV
Nymphenburg (Munich)	Wittlesbach	Museum	IV
Palais Edinburgh (Coburg)	Saxe-Coburg-Gotha	Chamber of Commerce	IV
Possenhofen	Wittelsbach	Private	IV
Rosenau (Rödental)	Saxe-Coburg-Gotha	Museum	IV
Roseninsel Casino (Lake Starnberg)	Wittelsbach	Museum	IV
Royal Villa (Berchtesgaden)	Wittelsbach	Private & Restaurant	IV
Schleissheim (Munich)	Wittelsbach	Museum	IV
Seehof (Memmelsdorf)	Prince-bishops Bamberg	Museum	IV
Seeon (Seeon-Seebruck)	Leuchtenberg	Conference centre	IV
St Emmeram (Regensburg)	Thurn und Taxis	Museum, Brewery, Offices	IV
Tegernsee	Wittelsbach	Private, School, Brewery	IV
Tittmoning	Prince-bishops Salzburg	Private & Museum	IV
Trausnitz (Landshut)	Wittelsbach	Museum	IV
Veste Coburg	Saxe-Coburg-Gotha	Museum	IV
Weissenstein (Pommersfelden)	Schönborn	Private with Museum	IV
Wildenwart (Frasdorf)	Wittelsbach	Private	IV

Berlin & Brandenburg

Altes Palais (Berlin)	Hohenzollern	University	I
Cecilienhof (Potsdam)	Hohenzollern	Museum & Hotel (closed)	I
Charlottenburg (Berlin)	Hohenzollern	Museum	I
Kronprinzenpalais (Berlin)	Hohenzollern	Events venue	I
Neues Palais (Potsdam)	Hohenzollern	Museum	I
New Pavilion (Berlin)	Hohenzollern	Museum	I
Paretz (Ketzin)	Hohenzollern	Museum	I
Rheinsberg	Hohenzollern	Museum	II
Sanssouci (Potsdam)	Hohenzollern	Museum	I

Hesse

Bad Homburg	Hesse-Homburg	Museum	I
Burgruine Königstein	Nassau	Museum	I
Darmstadt	Hesse-Darmstadt	University/empty, Museum	III
Friedberg	Hesse-Darmstadt	Government offices	III
Friedrichshof (Kronberg i/Taunus)	Hesse-Kassel	Hotel	I
Heiligenberg (Jugenheim)	Battenberg	Business centre, Museum	III
Kranichstein (Darmstadt)	Hesse-Darmstadt	Museum & Hotel	III
Kronberg	Lords of Kronberg	Museum	I
Luxembourg (Königstein i/Taunus)	Nassau	Law Court	I
Rosenhöhe (Darmstadt)	Hesse-Darmstadt	Gardens	III
Wilhelmshöhe (Kassel)	Hesse-Kassel	Museum	III
Wilhelmsthal (Calden)	Hesse-Kassel	Museum & Events venue	III
Wolfsgarten (Langen)	Hesse-Darmstadt	Private	III

Lower Saxony

Ahlden	Hannover	Auction house	I
Bevern	Brunswick-Bevern	Museum	III
Braunschweig	Brunswick-Wolfenbüttel	Shopping centre, Museum	II
Bückeburg	Schaumburg-Lippe	Museum	II
Celle	Hannover	Museum	I
Fallersleben (Wolfsburg)	Brunswick-Lüneburg	Museum	II
Herrenhausen (Hannover)	Hannover	Gardens	I
Jever	Anhalt-Zerbst	Museum	II
Kaiserpfalz (Goslar)	Holy Roman emperors	Museum	II
Marienburg (Pattensen)	Hannover	Museum	I
Oldenburg	Oldenburg	Museum	II
Pyrmont	Waldeck-Pyrmont	Museum	III
Rastede Palais	Oldenburg	Museum	II
Rastede Schloss	Oldenburg	Private	II
Little Richmond (Braunschweig)	Brunswick-Wolfenbüttel	Events venue & Park	II
Salzdahlum	Brunswick-Wolfenbüttel	Destroyed	II

Stadthagen	Holstein-Schaumburg	Government offices, Museum	II
Wolfenbüttel	Brunswick-Wolfenbüttel	Museum & School	II
Wolfsburg	Schulenburg-Wolfsburg	Cultural centre, Museum	II

Mecklenburg-Pomerania

Bad Doberan	Mecklenburg-Schwerin	Government offices	I
Blücher (Göhren-Lebbin)	Blücher	Hotel	II
Gamehl	von Stralendorff	Hotel	I
Gelbensande	Mecklenburg-Schwerin	Restaurant & Museum	I
Güstrow	Mecklenburg-Güstrow	Museum	I
Hohenzieritz	Mecklenburg-Strelitz	Offices & Museum	II
Ludwigslust	Mecklenburg-Schwerin	Museum	I
Mirow	Mecklenburg-Strelitz	Museum	II
Neustrelitz	Mecklenburg-Strelitz	Destroyed	II
Prinzenpalais (Bad Doberan)	Mecklenburg-Schwerin	Hotel	I
Schwerin	Mecklenburg-Schwerin	State Parliament, Museum	I
Burg Stargard	Mecklenburg-Strelitz	Museum, Hotel, Restaurant	II
Wiligrad (Löbstorf)	Mecklenburg-Schwerin	Artists' colony	I

North Rhine-Westphalia

Altena	von Mark	Museum	III
Augustusburg (Brühl)	Wittelsbach	Museum	III
Bensberg (Bergisch-Gladbach)	Wittelsbach	Hotel	III
Clemensruhe (Bonn)	Wittelsbach	University	III
Detmold	Lippe	Museum & Private	III
Electoral Palace (Bonn)	Wittelsbach	University	III
Falkenlust (Brühl)	Wittelsbach	Museum	III
Nordkirchen	von Plettenberg	University	III
Türnich (Kerpen)	von Hoensbroech	Market Garden, Café	III
Vischering (Lüdinghausen)	zu Vischering	Museum	III

Rhineland-Palatinate

Bathhouse Palace (Bad Ems)	Nassau-Diez	Hotel	III
Diez	Nassau-Diez	Youth hostel, Museum	III
Marksburg (Braubach)	Hesse/Nassau	Museum, Castles Assn	I
Oranienstein (Diez)	Nassau-Diez	Army base, Museum	III
Philippsburg (Braubach)	Hesse-Rheinfels	Library, Research Institute	I
Stolzenfels (Koblenz)	Hohenzollern	Museum	III
Vier Turme (Bad Ems)	von Thüngen	Government offices	III

Saxony

| Burg Stolpen | Wettin | Museum | I |
| Colditz | Wettin | Museum, Youth hostel | I |

Pillnitz (Dresden)	Wettin	Museum	I
Residenzschloss (Dresden)	Wettin	Museum	I
Rochlitz	Wettin	Museum	I
Taschenbergpalais (Dresden)	Wettin	Hotel	I

Saxony Anhalt

Bernburg	Anhalt-Bernburg	Museum	III
Luisium (Dessau)	Anhalt-Dessau	Museum, Park	III
Johannbau (Dessau)	Anhalt-Dessau	Museum, Café	III
Mosigkau	Anhalt-Dessau	Museum	III
Oranienbaum	Anhalt-Dessau	Museum, Park	III
Quedlinburg	Abbesses of Quedlinburg	Museum	III
Wörlitz	Anhalt-Dessau	Museum, Park	III

Schleswig-Holstein

Blomenburg (Selent)	von Blome	Empty/Development	II
Eutin	Holstein-Gottorf	Museum	II
Glücksburg	Holstein-Glücksburg	Museum	II
Gottorf	Holstein-Gottorf	Museum	II
Hemmelmark	Hohenzollern	Private	II
Husum	Holstein-Gottorf	Museum	II
Kiel	Hohenzollern	Concert hall	II
Salzau (Fargau-Pratjau)	von Blome	Empty	II

Thuringia

Altenstein (Bad Liebenstein)	Saxe-Meiningen	Under renovation, gardens	III
Belvedere (Weimar)	Saxe-Weimar-Eisenach	Museum	II
Elisabethenburg (Meiningen)	Saxe-Meiningen	Museum	III
Friedenstein (Gotha)	Saxe-Gotha-Altenburg	Museum, Gov't, Theatre	II
Heidecksburg (Rudolstadt)	Schwarzburg-Rudolstadt	Museum	II
Palais Weimar (Bad Liebenstein)	Saxe-Meiningen	Library	III
Reinhardsbrunn (Friedrichroda)	Saxe-Coburg-Gotha	Empty	II
Residenzschloss (Weimar)	Saxe-Weimar-Eisenach	Museum	II
Saalfeld	Saxe-Coburg-Saalfeld	Government offices	II
Schwarzburg	Schwarzburg-Rudolstadt	Under renovation, Museum	II
Wartburg (Eisenach)	Ludovingian	Museum, Hotel	III
Wilhelmsburg (Schmalkalden)	Hesse-Kassel	Museum	III

1. The list of schlösser is organised in alphabetical order by federal state and, within each state, in alphabetical order by schloss.
2. Where the schloss does not have the same name as the town or village in which it is located, the location is shown in brackets in the left hand column entitled 'Name'. For example, Callenberg is located in Coburg.
3. The column entitled 'Family' shows the name of the royal or noble family with which the author most associates the schloss. Schlösser that were part of a church state are listed under the title of the ruler of the state, for example, 'Prince-bishops of Bamberg'; and those that were imperial palaces are shown as 'Holy Roman Emperors'.
4. In the interests of space, a small number of family names have been abbreviated; for example Saxe-Coburg and Gotha has been abbreviated to Saxe-Coburg-Gotha.
5. Entries in the column entitled 'Current use' are based on the author's observations when visiting each schloss as part of researching the books. Major (but not necessarily all) uses are recorded.
6. The right hand side column called 'Book' indicates in which of the author's four books on schlösser a particular schloss is included – *Schloss* (I), *Schloss II* (II), *Schloss III* (III), and *Schloss in Bavaria* (IV).

APPENDIX C
CHARTS AND FAMILY TREES

1. Three generations of Schönborn church princes
2. Family tree for the Schenk Graf von Stauffenberg
3. The last Margrave of Brandenburg-Ansbach
4. Succession to the Duchy of Saxe-Coburg and Gotha
5. The Saxe-Coburg and Gotha thrones
6. The Princes of Thurn und Taxis in Regensburg
7. Family tree for the Dukes of Leuchtenberg
8. The house of Wittelsbach showing the branches included in this book
9. The Wittelsbach and Bavaria-Landshut
10. The Nine Dukes of Palatine-Neuburg
11. The Electors of Bavaria – from Maximilian I to Maximilian III Joseph
12. The Kings of Bavaria and the heads of house to the present day
13. The Dukes in Bavaria
14. The house of Wittelsbach today

1. THREE GENERATIONS OF SCHÖNBORN CHURCH PRINCES

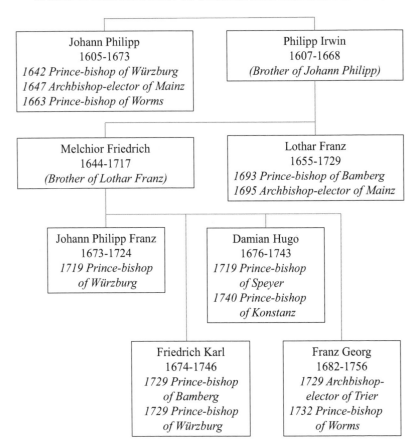

Johann Philipp
1605-1673
1642 Prince-bishop of Würzburg
1647 Archbishop-elector of Mainz
1663 Prince-bishop of Worms

Philipp Irwin
1607-1668
(Brother of Johann Philipp)

Melchior Friedrich
1644-1717
(Brother of Lothar Franz)

Lothar Franz
1655-1729
1693 Prince-bishop of Bamberg
1695 Archbishop-elector of Mainz

Johann Philipp Franz
1673-1724
1719 Prince-bishop
of Würzburg

Damian Hugo
1676-1743
1719 Prince-bishop
of Speyer
1740 Prince-bishop
of Konstanz

Friedrich Karl
1674-1746
1729 Prince-bishop
of Bamberg
1729 Prince-bishop
of Würzburg

Franz Georg
1682-1756
1729 Archbishop-
elector of Trier
1732 Prince-bishop
of Worms

2. FAMILY TREE FOR THE SCHENK GRAF VON STAUFFENBERG

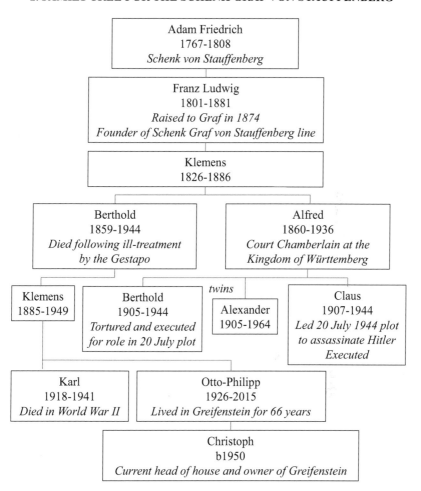

Adam Friedrich
1767-1808
Schenk von Stauffenberg

Franz Ludwig
1801-1881
Raised to Graf in 1874
Founder of Schenk Graf von Stauffenberg line

Klemens
1826-1886

Berthold
1859-1944
Died following ill-treatment
by the Gestapo

Alfred
1860-1936
Court Chamberlain at the
Kingdom of Württemberg

Klemens
1885-1949

Berthold
1905-1944
Tortured and executed
for role in 20 July plot

twins
Alexander
1905-1964

Claus
1907-1944
Led 20 July 1944 plot
to assassinate Hitler
Executed

Karl
1918-1941
Died in World War II

Otto-Philipp
1926-2015
Lived in Greifenstein for 66 years

Christoph
b1950
Current head of house and owner of Greifenstein

3. THE LAST MARGRAVE OF BRANDENBURG-ANSBACH

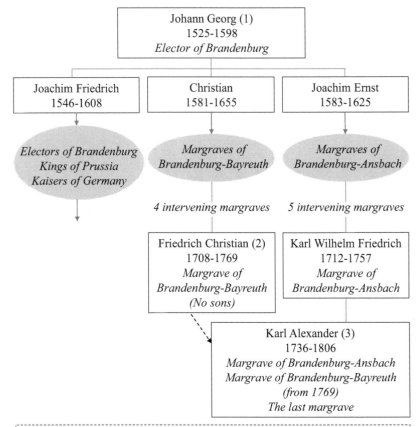

Johann Georg (1)
1525-1598
Elector of Brandenburg

Joachim Friedrich
1546-1608

Christian
1581-1655

Joachim Ernst
1583-1625

Electors of Brandenburg
Kings of Prussia
Kaisers of Germany

Margraves of
Brandenburg-Bayreuth

Margraves of
Brandenburg-Ansbach

4 intervening margraves

5 intervening margraves

Friedrich Christian (2)
1708-1769
Margrave of
Brandenburg-Bayreuth
(No sons)

Karl Wilhelm Friedrich
1712-1757
Margrave of
Brandenburg-Ansbach

Karl Alexander (3)
1736-1806
Margrave of Brandenburg-Ansbach
Margrave of Brandenburg-Bayreuth
(from 1769)
The last margrave

(1)   Chart shows the descent of the three Hohenzollern family branches from Elector Johann Georg . These branches were originally established by family decree of Elector Albrecht Achilles in 1473.
(2)   On the death of Friedrich Christian in 1769, the succession passed to his third cousin twice removed, Karl Alexander
(3)   In 1791, Karl Alexander sold Ansbach and Bayreuth to Prussia

4. SUCCESSION TO THE DUCHY OF SAXE-COBURG AND GOTHA

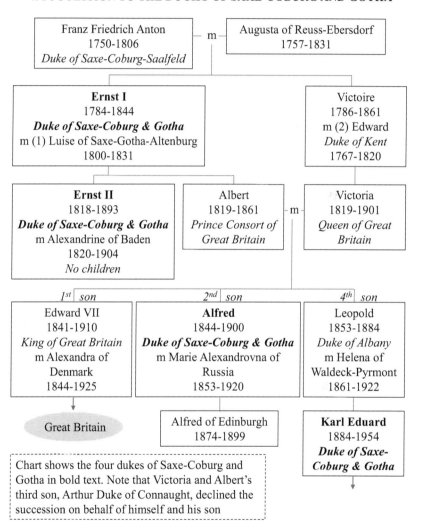

| Franz Friedrich Anton
1750-1806
Duke of Saxe-Coburg-Saalfeld | m | Augusta of Reuss-Ebersdorf
1757-1831 |

Ernst I
1784-1844
Duke of Saxe-Coburg & Gotha
m (1) Luise of Saxe-Gotha-Altenburg
1800-1831

Victoire
1786-1861
m (2) Edward
Duke of Kent
1767-1820

Ernst II
1818-1893
Duke of Saxe-Coburg & Gotha
m Alexandrine of Baden
1820-1904
No children

Albert
1819-1861
*Prince Consort of
Great Britain*

— m —

Victoria
1819-1901
*Queen of Great
Britain*

1ˢᵗ son

2ⁿᵈ son

4ᵗʰ son

Edward VII
1841-1910
King of Great Britain
m Alexandra of
Denmark
1844-1925

Alfred
1844-1900
Duke of Saxe-Coburg & Gotha
m Marie Alexandrovna of
Russia
1853-1920

Leopold
1853-1884
Duke of Albany
m Helena of
Waldeck-Pyrmont
1861-1922

Great Britain

Alfred of Edinburgh
1874-1899

Karl Eduard
1884-1954
***Duke of Saxe-
Coburg & Gotha***

Chart shows the four dukes of Saxe-Coburg and
Gotha in bold text. Note that Victoria and Albert's
third son, Arthur Duke of Connaught, declined the
succession on behalf of himself and his son

5. THE SAXE-COBURG AND GOTHA THRONES

Franz Friedrich Anton of	− married −	Augusta of
Saxe-Coburg-Saalfeld	1777	Reuss-Ebersdorf
1750-1806		1757-1831

Sophia 1778-1835	- married -	Emmanuel of Mensdorf-Pouilly 1777-1852	
Antoinette 1779-1824	- married -	Alexander of Württemberg 1771-1833	
Juliane 1781-1860	- married -	Constantine of Russia Brother of Tsar Alexander I 1779-1831	
Ernst 1784-1844	- married − (1)	Luise of Saxe-Gotha-Altenburg 1800-1831	⟶ (see entry for Victoire)
Ferdinand 1785-1851	- married -	Antoinette of Kohary 1797-1862	⟶ Portugal, Bulgaria, Brazil
Victoire 1786-1861	- married − (2)	Edward Duke of Kent 1767-1820	⟶ Great Britain, Prussia/Germany, Greece, Norway, Romania, Russia, Spain, Sweden, Yugoslavia
Marianne 1788-1794		*Died as a child*	
Leopold 1790-1865	- married − (2)	Louise of Orleans (France) 1812-1850	⟶ Belgium, Mexico, Italy, Luxembourg
Maximilian 1792-1793		*Died as a child*	

Chart shows the nine children of Franz Friedrich Anton and Augusta and the thrones occupied by their descendants. The name of the family changed to Saxe-Coburg and Gotha in 1826.

6. THE PRINCES OF THURN UND TAXIS IN REGENSBURG

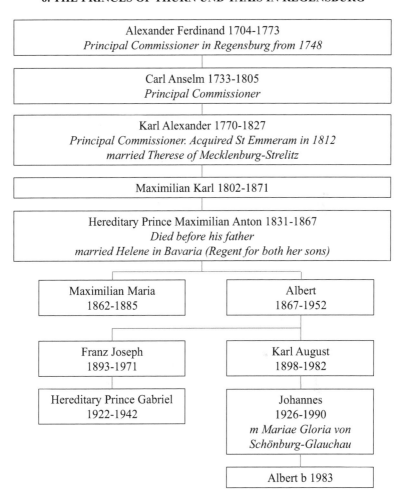

Alexander Ferdinand 1704-1773
Principal Commissioner in Regensburg from 1748

Carl Anselm 1733-1805
Principal Commissioner

Karl Alexander 1770-1827
*Principal Commissioner. Acquired St Emmeram in 1812
married Therese of Mecklenburg-Strelitz*

Maximilian Karl 1802-1871

Hereditary Prince Maximilian Anton 1831-1867
*Died before his father
married Helene in Bavaria (Regent for both her sons)*

Maximilian Maria
1862-1885

Albert
1867-1952

Franz Joseph
1893-1971

Karl August
1898-1982

Hereditary Prince Gabriel
1922-1942

Johannes
1926-1990
*m Mariae Gloria von
Schönburg-Glauchau*

Albert b 1983

7. FAMILY TREE FOR THE DUKES OF LEUCHTENBERG

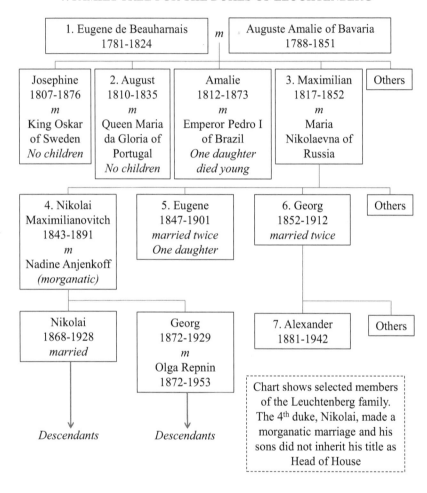

| 1. Eugene de Beauharnais 1781-1824 | *m* | Auguste Amalie of Bavaria 1788-1851 |

| Josephine 1807-1876 *m* King Oskar of Sweden *No children* | 2. August 1810-1835 *m* Queen Maria da Gloria of Portugal *No children* | Amalie 1812-1873 *m* Emperor Pedro I of Brazil *One daughter died young* | 3. Maximilian 1817-1852 *m* Maria Nikolaevna of Russia | Others |

| 4. Nikolai Maximilianovitch 1843-1891 *m* Nadine Anjenkoff *(morganatic)* | 5. Eugene 1847-1901 *married twice* *One daughter* | 6. Georg 1852-1912 *married twice* | Others |

| Nikolai 1868-1928 *married* | Georg 1872-1929 *m* Olga Repnin 1872-1953 | 7. Alexander 1881-1942 | Others |

Descendants   *Descendants*

Chart shows selected members of the Leuchtenberg family. The 4th duke, Nikolai, made a morganatic marriage and his sons did not inherit his title as Head of House

8. THE HOUSE OF WITTELSBACH SHOWING THE BRANCHES INCLUDED IN THIS BOOK

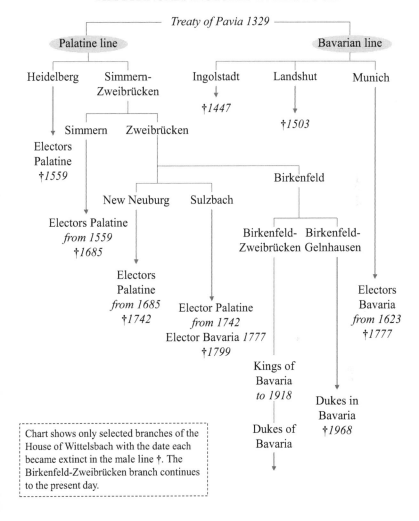

Chart shows only selected branches of the House of Wittelsbach with the date each became extinct in the male line †. The Birkenfeld-Zweibrücken branch continues to the present day.

9. THE WITTELSBACH AND BAVARIA-LANDSHUT

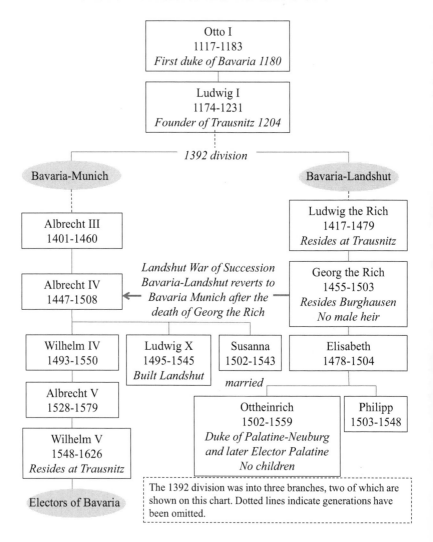

Otto I
1117-1183
First duke of Bavaria 1180

Ludwig I
1174-1231
Founder of Trausnitz 1204

1392 division

Bavaria-Munich

Bavaria-Landshut

Albrecht III
1401-1460

Ludwig the Rich
1417-1479
Resides at Trausnitz

*Landshut War of Succession
Bavaria-Landshut reverts to
← Bavaria Munich after the
death of Georg the Rich*

Albrecht IV
1447-1508

Georg the Rich
1455-1503
*Resides Burghausen
No male heir*

Wilhelm IV
1493-1550

Ludwig X
1495-1545
Built Landshut

Susanna
1502-1543

Elisabeth
1478-1504

married

Albrecht V
1528-1579

Ottheinrich
1502-1559
*Duke of Palatine-Neuburg
and later Elector Palatine
No children*

Philipp
1503-1548

Wilhelm V
1548-1626
Resides at Trausnitz

Electors of Bavaria

The 1392 division was into three branches, two of which are
shown on this chart. Dotted lines indicate generations have
been omitted.

10. THE NINE DUKES OF PALATINE-NEUBURG

---
1. Ottheinrich 1502-1505-1522-1559

Son of Elisabeth of Bavaria-Landshut and Rupprecht of the Palatine (Heidelberg branch).
The first duke when the principality was created in 1505; under a regency until 1522.
Builder of the three surviving renaissance wings at Schloss Neuburg.
In 1556 succeeded his uncle, Friedrich II, as elector of the Palatine.

---
2. Philipp 1503-1505-1522-1541-1548

Younger brother of Ottheinrich.
Ruled jointly with his brother 1522-1541.

---
3. Wolfgang 1526-1559-1569

Duke of the Zweibrücken branch of the Palatine line.
Distantly related to Ottheinrich (their great-great-grandfathers were brothers) and chosen
by him as the successor in Neuburg. (Note: the electorate of the Palatine went to the
Simmern branch on Ottheinrich's death.)
His sons, and their descendants, divided the Zweibrücken branch.

---
4. Philipp Ludwig 1547-1569-1614

Eldest son of Wolfgang.
Founder of the New Neuburg branch of the Palatine line.

---
5. Wolfgang Wilhelm 1578-1614-1653

Eldest son of Philipp Ludwig.
Converted to Catholicism following his marriage to the sister of the duke of Bavaria (and
catholicised Neuburg).
Through his mother, also inherited the duchies of Jülich and Berg.

6. Philipp Wilhelm 1615-1653-1690

Son of Wolfgang Wilhelm.
Built the baroque East Wing at Schloss Neuburg.
Became elector of the Palatine in 1685 on the extinction of the Simmern branch.

7. Johann Wilhelm (sometimes Jan Willem) 1658-1690-1716

Eldest son of Philipp Wilhelm.
Married twice but no children and succeeded by his brother.
Builder of Schloss Bensberg in Schloss III.

8. Karl III Philipp 1661-1716-1742

Younger brother of Johann Wilhelm.
The last male in the New Neuburg branch of the Palatine line.
Married three times but his only child was a daughter. His granddaughter married Karl Theodor of Sulzbach (see 9).

9. Karl Theodor 1724-1742-1799

From the Sulzbach branch of the Palatine line.
Descended from the younger son of Philipp Ludwig (see 4 above).
Succeeded as duke of Neuburg (Jülich and Cleves) and elector of the Palatine in 1742, on extinction of the New Neuburg branch.
Succeeded as elector of Bavaria in 1777, on the extinction of the Bavarian line of the House of Wittelsbach.

11. THE ELECTORS OF BAVARIA
FROM MAXIMILIAN I TO MAXIMILIAN III JOSEPH

> 1. Maximilian I 1573-1598-1623-1651
> Married (1) Elisabeth Renata of Lorraine 1595 (2) Maria Anna of Austria 1635

Succeeded as duke of Bavaria on the abdication of his father in 1598.
Promoted to elector of the Holy Roman Empire (in place of the Palatine line) in 1623.
Built the Old Palace at Schleissheim.

> 2. Ferdinand Maria 1636-1651-1679
> Married Henriette Adelaide of Savoy 1652

Henriette Adelaide built Borgo della Ninfe – Nymphenburg.

> 3. Maximilian II Emanuel 1662-1680-1726
> Married (1) Maria Antonia of Austria 1685 (2) Theresa Kunigunde Sobieski 1695

Regency 1679-1680. Exiled from Bavaria 1704-1715 in the War of the Spanish Succession.
Built Lustheim, Schleissheim New Palace, and Fürstenried.
Extended Nymphenburg and remodelled Dachau.

> 4. Karl Albrecht 1697-1726-1745
> Married Maria Amalia of Austria 1722

Holy Roman Emperor Karl VII 1742-1745.
Exiled from Bavaria 1742-1744 during the War of the Austrian Succession.
Built the Magdalenenklaus and Amalienburg at Nymphenburg.

> 5. Maximilian III Joseph 1727-1745-1777
> Married Maria Anna Sophia of Saxony 1747

The last ruler from the old Bavarian line of the House of Wittelsbach
On his death without an heir, the succession passed to Karl Theodor of Sulzbach.

12. THE KINGS OF BAVARIA AND THE HEADS OF HOUSE TO THE PRESENT DAY

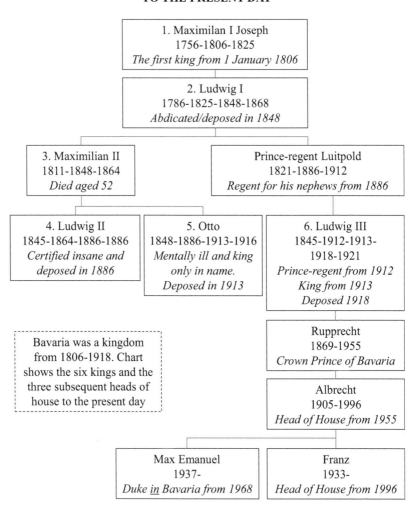

1. Maximilan I Joseph
1756-1806-1825
The first king from 1 January 1806

2. Ludwig I
1786-1825-1848-1868
Abdicated/deposed in 1848

3. Maximilian II
1811-1848-1864
Died aged 52

Prince-regent Luitpold
1821-1886-1912
Regent for his nephews from 1886

4. Ludwig II
1845-1864-1886-1886
Certified insane and deposed in 1886

5. Otto
1848-1886-1913-1916
Mentally ill and king only in name. Deposed in 1913

6. Ludwig III
1845-1912-1913-1918-1921
Prince-regent from 1912 King from 1913 Deposed 1918

Bavaria was a kingdom from 1806-1918. Chart shows the six kings and the three subsequent heads of house to the present day

Rupprecht
1869-1955
Crown Prince of Bavaria

Albrecht
1905-1996
Head of House from 1955

Max Emanuel
1937-
Duke in Bavaria from 1968

Franz
1933-
Head of House from 1996

13. THE DUKES IN BAVARIA

> **1. Wilhelm**
> 1752-1837
> *First duke in Bavaria 1799*

> **2. Pius August**
> 1786-1837

> **3. Maximilian (Max)**
> 1808-1888
> *m 1828*
> Ludovika of Bavaria
> 1808-1892

Others

Helene (Néné)	Elisabeth (Sisi)	**4. Karl Theodor**
1834-1890	1837-1898	1839-1909
m 1858	*m 1854*	*m (2) 1874*
Maximilian Anton	Emperor Franz Joseph	Marie José of Portugal
of Thurn und Taxis	of Austria	
	Sisi and Franz Joseph	**5. Ludwig Wilhelm**
	were first cousins – their	1884-1968
	mothers were sisters	*m 1917*
		Eleonore of Sayn-
		Wittgenstein-Berleburg

Chart shows the Dukes in Bavaria from creation in 1799 to the present day. Ludwig Wilhelm adopted the younger brother of Franz, Duke of Bavaria as his heir. Chart also shows the marriages of Néné and Sisi, duchesses in Bavaria.

by adoption

> **6. Max Emanuel**
> 1937-
> *Younger brother of Franz,*
> *Duke of Bavria*
> *Duke in Bavaria from 1968*

14. THE HOUSE OF WITTELSBACH TODAY

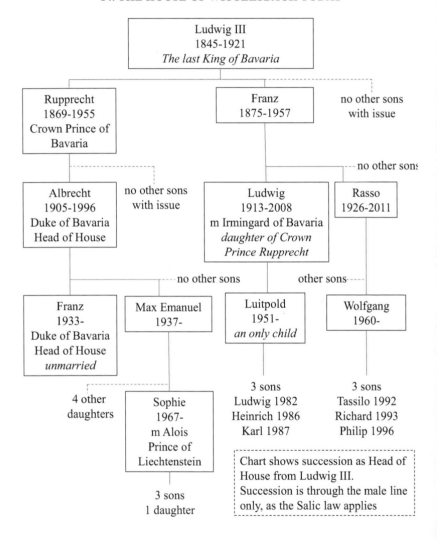

Ludwig III
1845-1921
The last King of Bavaria

Rupprecht
1869-1955
Crown Prince of
Bavaria

Franz
1875-1957

no other sons
with issue

Albrecht
1905-1996
Duke of Bavaria
Head of House

no other sons
with issue

Ludwig
1913-2008
m Irmingard of Bavaria
*daughter of Crown
Prince Rupprecht*

Rasso
1926-2011

no other sons

no other sons   other sons

Franz
1933-
Duke of Bavaria
Head of House
unmarried

Max Emanuel
1937-

Luitpold
1951-
an only child

Wolfgang
1960-

4 other
daughters

Sophie
1967-
m Alois
Prince of
Liechtenstein

3 sons
Ludwig 1982
Heinrich 1986
Karl 1987

3 sons
Tassilo 1992
Richard 1993
Philip 1996

3 sons
1 daughter

Chart shows succession as Head of
House from Ludwig III.
Succession is through the male line
only, as the Salic law applies

ILLUSTRATIONS

The illustrations noted below (by illustration number or page number) are reproduced by permission of the organisations or individuals listed. All other illustrations are from the author's collection.

2. Kaiserpfalz Forchheim.
10. Christoph Schenk Graf von Stauffenberg.
12. Christoph Schenk Graf von Stauffenberg.
13. Christoph Schenk Graf von Stauffenberg.
Pages 30 and 31. Kaiserpfalz Forchheim.
30. Stiftung der Herzog von Sachsen-Coburg und Gotha'schen Familie.
31. Stiftung der Herzog von Sachsen-Coburg und Gotha'schen Familie.
Pages 65 and 66. Kaeser Kompressoren.
65. Forderkries Roseninsel, Franz Jacob Kreuter, Wikipedia.
87. Wittelsbacher Ausgleichsfonds, Königliches Schloss Berchtesgaden.
88. Wittelsbacher Ausgleichsfonds, Königliches Schloss Berchtesgaden.
92. Wittelsbacher Ausgleichsfonds, Hohenschwangau.
Page 173. WGXC/Shutterstock.com.
94. Delpixel/Shutterstock.com.
97. Stadtarchiv, Stadt Füssen.

NOTES

Chapter 1

1. Theodor Hierneis, *The Monarch Dines: The Memories of Theodor Hierneis, One-time Cook at the Court of King Ludwig II of Bavaria* (London: Werner Laurie, 1954), 79-80.
2. This was Prince-bishop Lothar Franz von Schönborn – see New Residence Bamberg in chapter 2.

Chapter 2

1. Max H. von Freeden, *Schloss Weissenstein in Pommersfelden* (Königstein im Taunus: Verlag Langewiesche), 6.
2. Joachim Zeune, *Castles and Palaces: Germany* (Regensburg: Schmidt Verlag, 2004) 100.
3. Wikipedia, the free encyclopaedia. *Prince-Bishopric of Bamberg.* Retrieved 07/01/2017.
4. Different sources discuss different explanations. The schloss guidebook explains it as suicide (Erich Bachmann and Burkard von Roda, *Neue Residenz Bamberg* (Munich: Bayerische Verwaltung Der Staatlichen Schlösser Gärten und Seen, 1995) 87); Andrew Roberts in *Napoleon the Great,* (Penguin Books, 2015, 743) favours suicide but adds the possibility of accident due to the history of epilepsy; the website frenchempire.net adds some information in support of assassination (www.frenchempire. net/biographies/berthier).
5. Leonard Bower and Gordon Bolitho, *Otho I: King of Greece, a Biography* (London: Selwyn and Blount, 1939. Reprinted by *Royalty Digest* 2001) 242.
6. Coryne Hall, 'Crown Prince Rupprecht: the Best King Bavaria Never Had.' (*Eurohistory: the European Royal History Journal.* Volume 18.3 – June 2015, Part I), 2.
7. Hall, 'Crown Prince Rupprecht', Part 1, 3.
8. After Lothar Franz, the next prince-bishop was his nephew, Friedrich Karl von Schönborn (reigned 1729-1746). Friedrich Karl built the orangeries which flank the entrance to Seehof and now house the café.
9. She was the sister of Friedrich Karl von Schönborn.
10. Tour guide at Seehof.
11. Tour guide at Seehof.
12. Tour guide at Seehof.
13. The currency of Bavaria was the gulden or guilder until German unification in 1870; after which (in 1873) it became the Prussian mark. I have not found it possible to convert historic currency values into modern-day equivalents sums, and have therefore followed the approach of trying to put the figures

into some kind of context (for example that the grant from the emperor was sufficient to defray two-thirds of the building cost of Weissenstein).
14. Claude Arthaud, *Dream Palaces: Fantastic Houses and Their Treasures* (London: Thames and Hudson, 1973) 78.
15. Arthaud, *Dream Palaces*, 79.
16. Tour guide at Weissenstein.
17. Translation and explanation helpfully provided by Christoph Schenk Graf von Stauffenberg in email correspondence.
18. Monika Schenk Gräfin von Stauffenberg and Rainer Benker, *Schloss Greifenstein: Die Grafen Schenk von Stauffenberg* (Berlin: Verlag Monumente und Menschen) 12.
19. Schenk Gräfin von Stauffenberg and Benker, *Schloss Greifenstein*, 28.
20. BBC World Service online magazine 20 July 2014, interview with Berthold Schenk Graf von Stauffenberg (the son of Claus).
21. Birgit Friedal and G. Ulrich Grossman, *Nuremberg Imperial Palace* (Wartburg-Gesellschaft: 2006 (English edition)) 39.
22. Friedal and Grossman, *Nuremberg Imperial Palace*, 48.
23. Radu R. Florescu and Raymond T. McNally, *Dracula Prince of Many Faces: His Life and Times* (Boston: Little Brown and Company: 1989), 39-40.
24. Peter H. Wilson, *The Holy Roman Empire: A Thousand Years of Europe's History* (Allen Lane: 2016).
25. English handout for the guided tour.
26. Arno Störkel, *Christian Friedrich Karl Alexander Der Letzte Margrave von Ansbach-Bayreuth* (Ansbach: Wiedfeld & Mehl, 1995), 212.
27. Störkel, *Christian Friedrich Karl Alexander Der Letzte Margrave von Ansbach-Bayreuth*, 212.
28. Tour guide at Ansbach.
29. Tour guide at Ansbach.
30. Karl Alexander sold Brandenburg-Ansbach and also Brandenburg-Bayreuth, which he had inherited in 1769.
31. Oxford Dictionary of National Biography, Walpole, Corr., 34.132.
32. Jan Bondeson, 'Who was Kaspar Hauser?', *The Folio Book of Historical Mysteries* (London: The Folio Society: 2008), 208.

Chapter 3
1. Gilla Brückner, (*Experience Coburg*, Veitschöchheim: Elmer Hahn Verlag, 2011), 36. The emperor chose this name because the schloss had been built without the use of compulsory (bonded) labour.
2. Duke Ernst was a great restorer and re-modeller of schlösser. As well as the schlösser in this chapter, he also rebuilt Reinhardsbrunn in *Schloss II*.

3. This was the famous Prussian architect Karl Friedrich Schinkel who also worked on (as examples) the Rosenau and Stolzenfels (see *Schloss III*). Schinkel started his career as a painter and stage set designer.

4. Queen Victoria's Journal, RA VIC/MAIN/QVJ(W) Tuesday 19 August 1845 (Queen Victoria's drafts), retrieved 7 March 2017.

5. Victoria's mother was born Victoire of Saxe-Coburg-Saalfeld; she was the sister of Ernst I. Victoria's father was Edward, Duke of Kent. The Coburg wedding ceremony was under Lutheran rites. There was also a second ceremony under Church of England rites, in a double wedding with Kent's elder brother William, Duke of Clarence and Adelaide of Saxe-Meiningen, at Kew Palace outside London on 13 July 1818.

6. *The Loves of Prince Albert and Fair Victoria*,(Street Ballad of January 1940, John Johnson Collection, Bodleian Library, Oxford).

7. Getting married were two of Victoria's grandchildren – Grand Duke Ernst of Hesse-Darmstadt and Princess Victoria Melita of Saxe-Coburg and Gotha.

8. Richard Sotnick, *The Coburg Conspiracy: Victoria and Albert – Royal Plots and Manoeuvres* (Ephesus Publishing, 2008) 142-145.

9. Luise in a letter to Augusta von Studnitz of 21 September 1824, quoted in Sotnick, *The Coburg Conspiracy*, 147.

10. Queen Victoria's journal, RA VIC/MAIN/QVJ(W) Wednesday 20 August 1845 (Queen Victoria's drafts), retrieved 15 March 2017.

11. Stanley Weintraub, *Albert: Uncrowned King* (London: John Murray, 1997), 52.

12. Charlotte Zeepvat, 'The Queen and Uncle E' (*Royalty Digest: A Journal of Record*, July 2000) 2.

13. Diana Mandache, *Dearest Missy: The Correspondence Between Marie, Grand Duchess of Russia, Duchess of Edinburgh and of Saxe-Coburg and Gotha and her Daughter, Marie Crown Princess of Romania, 1879-1900* (Falkoping: Rosvall Royal Books, 2011), '...he has to leave the regiment ...', 349 (letter of 26 August 1898); '...his nasty illness ...' 368 (letter of 13 December 1898); 'A charming son, who pays his low life love affairs ...'337 (letter of 4 April 1898); 'You would be horrified if you saw him ...' 350 (letter of 7 September 1898).

14. Andreas, Prince of Saxe-Coburg and Gotha, *I Did It My Way...:The Memoirs of HH Prince Andreas of Saxe-Coburg and Gotha with Arturo E. Beéche* (East Richmond Heights (California): Eurohistory.com, 2015) 53.

15. Duke Alfred of Saxe-Coburg and Gotha was Queen Victoria's second son and Leopold, Duke of Albany was her fourth (and youngest) son. The third son, Arthur Duke of Connaught, declined the Coburg succession on behalf of himself and his only son.

16. Andreas, Prince of Saxe-Coburg and Gotha, *I Did It My Way*, 71.
17. Andreas, Prince of Saxe-Coburg and Gotha, *I Did It My Way*, 64-71.
18. See Huburtus Büschel, *Hitler's Adliger Diplomat: Der Herzog von Coburg und das Dritte Reich* (published 2016 in German).
19. Klaus Weschenfelder, *Art Collections Veste Coburg* (Regensburg: Schnell &Steiner, 2008) 26.
20. Marie, Queen of Romania, *The Story of My Life: Volume I*, quoted in Charlotte Zeepvat, 'The Queen and Uncle E.' (*Royalty Digest: A Journal of Record*, July 2000), 7. Marie was the daughter of Duke Alfred.
21. Queen Victoria's Journal, RA VIC/MAIN/QVJ(W) Monday 1 October 1860 (Princess Beatrice's copies), retrieved 13 March 2017.
22. Cecil Woodham-Smith, *Queen Victoria Her Life and Times: Volume I 1819-1861* (London: Hamish Hamilton, 1972), 402. (And Albert was quite correct.)
23. William Mead Lalor, 'The Grand Duchess Anna Feodorovna, Poor Dear Aunt Julie' (*Royalty Digest: A Journal of Record*, July 1996), 11.
24. Lalor, 'The Grand Duchess Anna Feodorovna', 12.
25. A very interesting article by Richard Thornton in Royalty Digest Quarterly (2008 volume 2, 39), called 'Prince Albert's sister and other shady Coburgs', covers Juliane's life after she left Russia. She had a child from each of two relationships with the heads of her household. The children (a boy and a girl) were adopted. After years of separation, her husband Constantine tried for a reconciliation (perhaps because it was apparent that Juliane was fertile and Russia needed an heir) but she refused.
26. Descendants of Leopold occupied three more thrones. His daughter Charlotte was the doomed empress of Mexico from 1863-1867; his great-granddaughter Marie José was the queen of Italy for a month in 1946 before the monarchy was abolished; and his great-great-granddaughter Josephine Charlotte became Grand Duchess of Luxembourg, when her husband succeeded in 1964.
27. Augusta, Duchess of Saxe-Coburg-Saalfeld. *In Napoleonic Days: Extracts from the Private Diary of Augusta, Duchess of Saxe-Coburg-Saalfeld, Queen Victoria's Maternal Grandmother, 1806-1821: Selected and Translated by H.R.H. The Princess Beatrice*. London: John Murray, 1941, 192.
28. In 1914, on the outbreak of World War I, Victoria and Albert's grandchildren sat on, or were in waiting for, the following thrones (the women as consorts) – Germany (Kaiser Wilhelm II), Great Britain (King George V), Greece (Queen Sophie), Norway (Queen Maud), Romania (Queen Marie), Russia (Tsarina Alexandra), Spain (Queen Victoria Eugenie), and Sweden (Crown Princess Margareta). In addition, in 1922 a great-granddaughter (Queen Marie) married the king of Yugoslavia.

29. Ferdinand's father was another son of Duke Franz Friedrich Anton and was also called Ferdinand. In 1864 a grandson of Ferdinand senior (called Gaston) married the heiress to the throne of Brazil. She acted as regent for her father when he was absent from the country but the monarchy was abolished before she came to the throne. In 1887 another grandson (yet another Ferdinand) was elected sovereign prince of Bulgaria and later proclaimed himself tsar.

30. Andreas, Prince of Saxe-Coburg and Gotha, *I Did It My Way...:The Memoirs of HH Prince Andreas of Saxe-Coburg and Gotha with Arturo E. Beéche* (East Richmond Heights (California): Eurohistory.com, 2015).

31. Augusta, Duchess of Saxe-Coburg-Saalfeld, *In Napoleonic Days*, 13 March 1817, 177.

Chapter Four

1. Princess Mariae Gloria Thurn und Taxis and Todd Eberle, *House of Thurn und Taxis* (New York: Skira Rizzoli, 2015), 9.

2. Thurn und Taxis and Eberle, *House of Thurn und Taxis*, 19. In his foreword to the book, Todd Eberle refers to the *Vanity Fair* article on the sixtieth birthday party of Prince Johannes, which coined the nickname 'Princess TNT'. Another name given to the princess by the press was 'Princess Punk'.

3. The book is *House of Thurn und Taxis* (New York: Skira Rizzoli, 2015).

4. Peter Styra, *Das Haus Thurn und Taxis: Gesamtgeschichte mit Stammfolge* (Werle (Westphaen): Borde Verlag Werl, 2016), 18.

5. Styra, *Das Haus Thurn und Taxis*, 20.

6. Styra, *Das Haus Thurn und Taxis*, 9.

Chapter Five

1. Wilhelm Heizer, *History and Art Landshut* (Tourist Office of Landshut, 1993), 26.

2. Julia Ricker, *Georg der Reiche* (Haus der Bayerischen Geschichte www.hdbg.de, 2015, translated by Gert-Jürgen Frisch) gives the sum spent as 69,766 florins. A florin was another name for a guilder or gulden.

3. Heizer, *History and Art Landshut*, 28.

4. Heizer, *History and Art Landshut*, 31.

5. Susan Maxwell, 'A Marriage Commemorated in the Stairway of Fools', *The Sixteenth Century Journal* (Vol 36, No 3, Fall 2005), 721. Maxwell gives this as a rough translation of a phrase in a letter from the Bavarian court composer Orlando di Lasso.

6. The distance is 1051 metres.

7. Joachim Zeune, *Castles and Palaces: Germany* (Regensburg: Schmidt Verlag,

2004), 90.

8. *Burghausen: Welt Längste Burg* (Burghausen: Burghauser Touristik, 2015, English edition), 17. Ricker, *Georg der Reiche*, says that historians have valued the treasure at a million guilders.

9. Lotte Lahr, *Burghausen: Europe's Longest Castle* (Altötting: Gebr. Geiselberger, 2011), 21.

10. When the church states were dissolved in 1803, the area was briefly part of a short-lived state called the Electorate of Salzburg.

11. Duke Ludwig IV of Bavaria (1282-1347) was the Holy Roman emperor, known as Ludwig the Bavarian, from 1314 until his death. The archbishop of Salzburg at the time was Friedrich III von Leibnitz, reigned 1315-1338.

12. A leaflet in English from the information office in the town of Tittmoning gives the figure as 5500 Salzburg pfennigs. The pfennig was the currency of the Archbishopric of Salzburg.

13. Duke Maximilian of Bavaria (1573-1651), from 1623 Elector Maximilian I. The archbishop of Salzburg at this time was Markus Sittikus von Hohenems, reigned 1612-1619.

14. Elector Karl Albrecht of Bavaria (1697-1745) was the Holy Roman Emperor Karl VII from 1742 until his death. Karl (and other great powers) tried to take advantage of the succession of Empress Maria Theresa of Austria (the only female Hapsburg ruler) in 1740 to seize parts of Austrian territory.

15. The price paid was 2,210 guilders (leaflet in English from the information office in the town of Tittmoning).

16. Peter Keller, *Johann Michael Rottmayr (1654-1730)im Salzburger Land und im Rupertiwinkel* (Dom Museum zu Salzburg, Stadt Laufen an der Salzach), 30 has this illustration.

17. The three other spellings used in various sources are (1) Otto Heinrich (I understand this is how he was christened) (2) Ottoheinrich and (3) Otto-Heinrich. I decided to use Ottheinrich in this book because this spelling is used at Schloss Neuburg and also by Haus der Bayerischen Geschichte (the House of Bavarian History) www.hdbg.de.

18. Ottheinrich's younger brother was Philipp (1503-1548). Palatinate-Neuburg was under the regency of their father's family until 1522; after which the brothers ruled it jointly. In 1535 the duchy was divided between them until a few years later, in 1541, everything reverted to Ottheinrich. (I have not been able to find more information about these events.)

19. She married first Margrave Kasimir of Brandenburg-Kulmbach; he died in 1527 and Susanna married Ottheinrich in 1529.

20. Haus der Bayerischen Geschichte (www.hdbg.de) *Herzogin von Pfalz-Neuburg Susanna.*

21. Brigitte Langer (Edited by), *Schloss Neuburg an der Donau* (Munich: Bayerische Verwaltung Der Staatlichen Schlösser Gärten und Seen, 2007), 73.

22. Peter O. Krückmann, *The Wittelsbach Palaces: From Landshut and Höchstädt to Munich* (Munich: Prestel, 2001), 50-51.

23. Krückmann, *The Wittelsbach Palaces*, 52.

24. Audio-guide at Schleissheim New Palace.

25. Luisa Hager, *Schloss Schleissheim* (Königstein im Taunus: Karl Robert Langewiesche Nachfolger Hans Köster, 1974) page X (roman numerals are used for the page numbers).

26. Isabella Schinzel and Eric-Oliver Mader, *Nymphenburg Palace: Pleasure Palace of the Wittelsbachs* (Hamburg: TopSpot Guide) 50, puts the size of the debt at twenty-five million guilders, roughly equivalent to ten times the elector's annual income.

27. Brigitte Langer and Gerhard Hojer (Edited by), *Nymphenburg Palace, Park, and Pavilions* (Munich: Bayerische Verwaltung Der Staatlichen Schlösser Gärten und Seen, 2007) 17.

28. William Mead Lalor, 'The King Who Loved Beauty: The Story of Ludwig I of Bavaria' (*Royalty Digest: A Journal of Record*, August 1997), 49.

29. Mary S. Lovell, *A Scandalous Life: The Biography of Jane Digby el Mezrab*, (London: Richard Cohen Books, 1995), 101 and plate 20 opposite 176.

30. The English audio guide at Nymphenburg says she pretended to faint; Henry Channon, *The Ludwigs of Bavaria* (London: Methuen & Co, 1934), 36, says she bared her bosom.

31. English audio guide at Nymphenburg.

32. Channon, *The Ludwigs of Bavaria*, 48.

33. Greg King, *The Mad King: The Life and Times of Ludwig II of Bavaria* (London: Arum Press, 1997), 228. King states that ex-king Ludwig I's pension was half a million guilders, out of the total civil list voted to his grandson, King Ludwig II, of two million guilders.

34. Schinzel and Mader, *Nymphenburg Palace*, 50.

35. Langer and Hojer, *Nymphenburg Palace*, 123.

36. This wedding was celebrated in style with two weeks of events at the Munich Residenz, Nymphenburg, Schleissheim, and Dachau.

37. Schinzel and Mader, *Nymphenburg Palace*,18.

38. Channon, *The Ludwigs of Bavaria*, 228.

39. Langer and Hojer, *Nymphenburg Palace*, 148.

40. Langer and Hojer, *Nymphenburg Palace*, 173.

Chapter 6

1. Elmar D. Schmid (Edited by), *Die Roseninsel im Starnberger See* (Munich: Bayerische Verwaltung Der Staatlichen Schlösser Gärten und Seen, 2011), 112-114.
2. Martha Schad, *Ludwig II* (Munich: dtv, 2016) 49.
3. Greg King, *The Mad King: The Life and Times of Ludwig II of Bavaria* (London: Arum Press, 1997) 43.
4. Schad, *Ludwig II*, 28, says that in 1865 (the year following his accession), he was in Munich for only sixty-eight days.
5. Schmid, *Die Roseninsel*, 67.
6. Schad, *Ludwig II*, 68.
7. King, *The Mad King*, 167, quoting from Gottfried von Bohm, *Ludwig II, König von Bayern*, 2:402.
8. Schad, *Ludwig II*, 58-59; also Elisabeth Von Hagenow, Luitgard Löw and Andreas von Majewski (Edited by), *Museum of the Bavarian Kings Hohenschwangau: Catalogue on Behalf of the Wittelsbacher Ausgleichsfonds*, 77. The young man was Edgar Hanfstaengl and he was the son of the photographer Franz Hanfstaengl.
9. This is my husband's translation of the German poem from Schmid, *Die Roseninsel*, 82.
10. Desmond Chapman-Huston, *Bavarian Fantasy: The Story of Ludwig II* (London: John Murray, 1955) 72.
11. Schmid, *Die Roseninsel*, 71-74.
12. In 1818, Ludwig's great-grandfather, King Maximilian I Joseph, was the first monarch of a large German state to grant his subjects a constitution similar to that in other Western European countries. Von Hagenow, *Museum of the Bavarian Kings Hohenschwangau*, 68.
13. Elmar D. Schmid and Gerhard Hojer (Edited by), *Linderhof Palace* (Munich: Bayerische Verwaltung Der Staatlichen Schlösser Gärten und Seen, 2006) 8. Louis XVI was the three times great-grandson of Louis XIV.
14. Theodor Hierneis, *The Monarch Dines: The Memories of Theodor Hierneis, One-time Cook at the Court of King Ludwig II of Bavaria* (London: Werner Laurie, 1954) 38.
15. In 1865 Ludwig was forced by his government to exile Richard Wagner from Bavaria, very much against the king's own wishes; in 1866 he was required to support Austria against Prussia in the Seven Weeks' War, when his own inclination was for peace; in 1867 his engagement to Duchess Sophie in Bavaria failed.

16. King, *The Mad King,* 26.

17. Schmid and Hojer, *Linderhof Palace,* 9.

18. K. Höldrich and G. Schinzel-Penth, *Castle Linderhof: Royal Palace and Parkland* (Hamburg: TopSpot Guide) 20.

19. Theodor Hierneis. *The Monarch Dines: The Memories of Theodor Hierneis, One-time Cook at the Court of King Ludwig II of Bavaria.* London: Werner Laurie, 1954.

20. King, *The Mad King,* 234.

21. Hierneis, *The Monarch Dines,* 31-33.

22. From the oil painting of 1869 by Friedrich Wilhelm Pfeiffer.

23. Elmar D. Schmid and Kerstin Knirr (Edited by), *Herrenchiemsee* (Munich: Bayerische Verwaltung Der Staatlichen Schlösser Gärten und Seen, 2007) 18.

24. Herreninsel is a large and level site, 240 hectare or 593 acres in size. Ludwig II must also have been attracted by the seclusion of the island.

25. Schmid and Knirr, *Herrenchiemsee,* 69-70.

26. Schad, *Ludwig II,* 43.

27. Peter O. Krückmann, *The Land of Ludwig II: The Royal Castles and Residences in Upper Bavaria and Swabia* (Munich: Prestel, 2012) 44.

28. Guided tour at Herrenchiemsee.

29. Schmid and Knirr, *Herrenchiemsee,* 104.

30. King, *The Mad King,* 243. Greg King gives his source as Otto Zareck, *The Tragic Idealist: Ludwig II of Bavaria* (New York: Harper, 1939), 220.

31. *Designs for the Dream King: The Castles and Palaces of Ludwig II of Bavaria* (London: Debrett's Peerage for the Victoria and Albert Museum, London and the Cooper-Hewitt Museum, New York, Exhibition Catalogue, 1978) 15. This gives the cost figures in marks (the currency of Bavaria from 1873) as Neuschwanstein 6,180,047, Linderhof 8,460,937, and Herrenchiemsee 16,579,674.

32. King, *The Mad King,* debt figure 247; income figure 228. King gives the income figure as two million guilders. I have converted this at the rate used when the currency changed in 1873 (one guilder to 1.7 marks) – see Wikipedia: Bavarian gulden; retrieved 24/06/2017. A different source (Julius Desing, *King Ludwig II: His Life – His End.* Verlag Wilhelm Kienberger) puts a similar figure on the debt (13 million marks) but gives a higher figure (5.5 million) for Ludwig II's annual income.

33. King, *The Mad King,* 249.

34. Schad, *Ludwig II,* 121.

35. Copy of print F.J. Beich 1722/23, original in Schloss Nymphenburg. Copy of plan of reconstruction and re-planning by Carl von Effner around 1890.

36. *A Brief Overview of Our History*. Information in English from Schloss Fürstenried.
37. Paul B. Bernard, *Joseph II and Bavaria: Two Eighteenth century Attempts at German Unification* (The Hague: Martinus Nijhoff, 1965) 118.
38. Chapman-Huston, *Bavarian Fantasy*, 166-7, quoting a letter dated 6 January 1871 from Ludwig to Frau von Leonrod (his ex-governess).
39. Peter Galloway, 'The Twilight King: Otto of Bavaria.' *Royalty Digest: A Journal of Record*, April 2004, includes two photos of the king during his confinement at Fürstenried on pages 301 and 302.
40. Extracts from the magazine *Home Chat* of 10 April and 1 May 1909, reprinted in 'Oldest Monarch', *Royalty Digest: A Journal of Record*, October 1991, 123.
41. Schad, *Ludwig II*, 128.
42. Schad, *Ludwig II*, 130.
43. Lothar Altmann, *Kloster Seeon: The Centre for Culture and Education of Upper Bavaria and its Monastic Roots* (Lindenberg in Allgäu: Kunstverlag Josef Fink, 2011) 45-48.
44. Zoia Belyakova, *Honour and Fidelity: The Russian Dukes of Leuchtenberg* (St Petersburg: Logos publishers, 2010) 81.
45. Belyakova, *Honour and Fidelity*, 84.
46. Peter Kurth, *Anastasia: The Life of Anna Anderson* (London: Jonathan Cape, 1983) 165. This is a quote from Grand Duke Andrei about a letter he received from Georg 'He wrote to me from Paris that ...'.
47. Vera Green and Victoria Hughes, *Almost Anastasia the Life of Franziska Schanzkowsky* (Everglades: Whistling Swan Press, 2015) 156.
48. English handout for the German guided tour at Schloss Berchtesgaden, 1.
49. Holger Kempkens, *Augustusburg Palace, Brühl* (Berlin and Munich: Deutscher Kunstverlag, 2010), 7.
50. Coryne Hall, 'Crown Prince Rupprecht: the Best King Bavaria Never Had.' *Eurohistory: the European Royal History Journal*. Volume 18.3 – June 2015 (Part I), 3-4. Antonia's eldest sister, Grand Duchess Marie Adelaide, had to abdicate over her alleged pro-German leanings and it was not until the next sister, who became Grand Duchess Charlotte, had produced an heir that it was felt safe for Antonia to marry Rupprecht.
51. Irmingard, Prinzessin von Bayern. *Jugend-Erinnerungen [Memories of Youth] 1923-1950*. Eos Verlag U. Druck, 2000.
52. Henry Channon, *The Ludwigs of Bavaria* (London: Methuen & Co, 1934) 3-4.
53. Hagenow, Löw and von Majewski, *Museum of the Bavarian Kings Catalogue*, 139.
54. Hagenow, Löw and von Majewski, *Museum of the Bavarian Kings Catalogue*, 624. Hall, 'Crown Prince Rupprecht', *Eurohistory* August 2015 (Part II), 6.

Chapter 7

1. Gisela Haasen, *Hohenschwangau Castle* (Munich: Wittlesbacher Ausgleichsfonds, 2013) 19.
2. Handout with English translation for the exhibition in the Royal Lodge at Linderhof (see chapter 6). The quote is said to be from Maximilian's memoirs.
3. Haasen, *Hohenschwangau Castle*, 15, in a letter to Maximilian from Quaglio.
4. Alice Arnold-Becker, *Hohenschwangau Castle: The Murals of a Mountain Palace* (Augsburg: Alice Arnold-Becker, 2015) 11.
5. Elisabeth Von Hagenow, Luitgard Löw and Andreas von Majewski (Edited by), *Museum of the Bavarian Kings Hohenschwangau: Catalogue on Behalf of the Wittelsbacher Ausgleichsfonds*, 46.
6. Von Hagenow, Löw and von Majewski, *Museum of the Bavarian Kings Hohenschwangau: Catalogue*, 39.
7. Torquata Tasso (1544-1595), Arnold-Becker, *Hohenschwangau Castle*, 54.
8. Desmond Chapman-Huston, *Bavarian Fantasy: The Story of Ludwig II* (London: John Murray, 1955), 55, suggests syphilis. Christian Misniks, *Hohenschwangau Castle* (Oberammergau: Linderbichl Verlag, 2005), 52, mentions a severs bacterial infection called Rotlauf in German (in English Swine Erysipelas or more commonly St Anthony's Fire).
9. Joachim Zeune, *Das Hohes Schloss in Füssen* (Regensburg: Schnell & Steiner, 2010), 9.
10. It is thought that St Mang (or Magnus) arrived in Fussen around 730/740 AD (Zeune, *Das Hohes Schloss in Füssen*, 4) and died here in 750 AD (information at Hohes Schloss Füssen).
11. Zeune, *Das Hohes Schloss in Füssen*, 6.

BIBLIOGRAPHY

Altmann, Lothar. *Kloster Seeon: The Centre for Culture and Education of Upper Bavaria and its Monastic Roots.* Lindenberg in Allgäu: Kunstverlag Josef Fink, 2011.

Andreas, Prince of Saxe-Coburg and Gotha. *I Did It My Way ... : The Memoirs of HH Prince Andreas of Saxe-Coburg and Gotha with Arturo E. Beéche.* East Richmond Heights (California): Eurohistory.com, 2015.

Arnold-Becker, Alice. *Hohenschwangau Castle: The Murals of a Mountain Palace.* Augsburg: Alice Arnold-Becker, 2015.

Art for Spaces: Spaces for Art. Interior Spaces as Works of Art – Discovered in Palaces, Castles and Monasteries in Germany. Regensburg: Schnell and Steiner, 2005.

Arthaud, Claude. *Dream Palaces: Fantastic Houses and Their Treasures.* London: Thames and Hudson, 1973.

Augusta, Duchess of Saxe-Coburg-Saalfeld. *In Napoleonic Days: Extracts from the Private Diary of Augusta, Duchess of Saxe-Coburg-Saalfeld, Queen Victoria's Maternal Grandmother, 1806-1821: Selected and Translated by H.R.H. The Princess Beatrice.* London: John Murray, 1941.

Bachmann, Erich and Albrecht Miller. *Imperial Castle Nuremberg: Official Guide.* Munich: Bayerische Verwaltung Der Staatlichen Schlösser, Gärten und Seen. 1994.

Bachmann, Erich and Burkard von Roda. *Neue Residenz Bamberg.* Munich: Bayerische Verwaltung Der Staatlichen Schlösser Gärten und Seen, 1995.

Beéche, Arturo E. *The Coburgs of Europe: The Rise and Fall of Queen Victoria and Prince Albert's European Family.* East Richmond Heights (California): Eurohistory.com, 2013.

Belyakova, Zoia. *Honour and Fidelity: The Russian Dukes of Leuchtenberg.* St Petersburg: Logos publishers, 2010.

Bernard, Paul B. *Joseph II and Bavaria: Two Eighteenth Century Attempts at German Unification.* The Hague: Martinus Nijhoff, 1965.

Bolitho, Hector (Edited by). *The Prince Consort and His Brother: Two Hundred New Letters.* London: Cobden-Sanderson, 1933.

Bondeson, Jan. 'Who was Kaspar Hauser?', *The Folio Book of Historical Mysteries.* London: The Folio Society: 2008.

Bower, Leonard and Gordon Bolitho. *Otho I: King of Greece, a Biography.* London: Selwyn and Blount, 1939. Reprinted by *Royalty Digest* 2001.

Brückner, Gilla. *Experience Coburg.* Veitschöchheim: Elmer Hahn Verlag, 2011.

Brunner, Herbert and Lorenz Seelig. *Coburg Ehrenburg Palace: Official Guide.* Munich: Bayerische Verwaltung Der Staatlichen Schlösser Gärten und Seen, 1984.

Burghausen: Welt Längste Burg. Burghausen: Burghauser Touristik, 2015 (English edition).

Burkhart, Guido and Franz Rappel. *Berchtesgaden Castle.* Hamburg: Discover Guides, 2007.

Channon, Henry. *The Ludwigs of Bavaria.* London: Methuen & Co, 1934.

Chapman-Huston, Desmond. *Bavarian Fantasy: The Story of Ludwig II.* London: John Murray, 1955.

Designs for the Dream King: The Castles and Palaces of Ludwig II of Bavaria. London: Debrett's Peerage for the Victoria and Albert Museum, London and the Cooper-Hewitt Museum, New York, Exhibition Catalogue, 1978.

Friedal, Birgit and G. Ulrich Grossman. *Nuremberg Imperial Palace.* Wartburg-Gesellschaft: 2006 (English edition).

Friedrich, Verena. *Burgen und Schlösser in Franken.* Veitshöcheim: Elmar Hahn Verlag.

Galloway, Peter. 'The Twilight King: Otto of Bavaria.' *Royalty Digest: A Journal of Record,* April 2004, 298.

Gehrlein, Thomas. *Das Haus Schönborn: Mit Seinen Linien Buchheim, Wiesentheid und Schönborn.* Werle (Westphalia): Börde-Verlag, 2012.

Götz, Ernst and Brigitte Langer. *Schlossanlage Scheissheim.* Munich: Bayerische Verwaltung Der Staatlichen Schlösser Gärten und Seen, 2009.

Graf Pfeil, Christoph. *Residenz Ansbach mit Hofgarten und Orangerie.* Munich: Bayerische Verwaltung Der Staatlichen Schlösser: 2005.

Green, Vera and Victoria Hughes. *Almost Anastasia the Life of Franziska Schanzkowsky.* Everglades: Whistling Swan Press, 2015.

Hager, Luisa. *Schloss Schleissheim.* Königstein im Taunus: Karl Robert Langewiesche Nachfolger Hans Köster, 1974.

Hall, Coryne. 'Crown Prince Rupprecht: The Best King Bavaria Never Had.' *Eurohistory: the European Royal History Journal.* Volume 18.3 – June 2015 (Part I), Volume 18.4 – August 2015 (Part II).

Haasen, Gisela. *Hohenschwangau Castle.* Munich: Wittlesbacher Ausgleichsfonds, 2013.

Heizer, Wilhelm. *History and Art Landshut.* Tourist Office of Landshut, 1993.

Hierneis, Theodor. *The Monarch Dines: The Memories of Theodor Hierneis, One-time Cook at the Court of King Ludwig II of Bavaria.* London: Werner Laurie, 1954.

Hiley, Ann. *Regensburg: A Short History.* Regensburg: Verlag Friedrich Pustet: 2013.

Hoffman, Peter. *Stauffenberg: A Family History, 1905-1944.* Cambridge: Cambridge University Press, 1995.

Höldrich K. and G. Schinzel-Penth. *Castle Linderhof: Royal Palace and Parkland.* Hamburg: TopSpot Guide.

Keller, Peter. *Johann Michael Rottmayr (1654-1730) im Salzburger Land und im Rupertiwinkel.* Dom Museum zu Salzburg, Stadt Laufen an der Salzach.

King, Greg. *The Mad King: The Life and Times of Ludwig II of Bavaria.* London: Arum Press, 1997.

King, Greg. 'The Mad King's Other Empress: Ludwig II and Maria Alexandrovna of Russia.' *Eurohistory: The European Royal History Journal.* East Richmond Heights, California: Issue CXII, Volume 19.4, Winter 2016, 21.

Krückmann, Peter O. *The Wittelsbach Palaces: From Landshut and Höchstädt to Munich.* Munich: Prestel, 2001.

Krückmann, Peter O. *The Land of Ludwig II: The Royal Castles and Residences in Upper Bavaria and Swabia.* Munich: Prestel, 2012.

Krückmann, Peter O. *Residences of the Prince-Bishops in Franconia: the Courts of the Schönborns and of Other Prince-Bishops Along the River Main.* Munich: Prestel, 2002.

Kurth, Peter. *Anastasia: The Life of Anna Anderson.* London: Jonathan Cape, 1983.

Lahr, Lotte. *Burghausen: Europe's Longest Castle.* Altötting: Gebr. Geiselberger, 2011.

Langer, Brigitte (Edited by). *Burg Zu Burghausen.* Munich: Bayerische Verwaltung Der Staatlichen Schlösser Gärten und Seen, 2011.

Langer, Brigitte (Edited by). *Burg Trausnitz Landshut.* Munich: Bayerische Verwaltung Der Staatlichen Schlösser Gärten und Seen, 2013.

Langer, Brigitte (Edited by). *Schloss Neuburg an der Donau.* Munich: Bayerische Verwaltung Der Staatlichen Schlösser Gärten und Seen, 2015.

Langer, Brigitte and Gerhard Hojer (Edited by). *Nymphenburg Palace, Park and Pavilions.* Munich: Bayerische Verwaltung Der Staatlichen Schlösser Gärten und Seen, 2007.

Leuchtenberg: Zeit des Adels in Seeon und Stein: Katalog zur Ausstellung im Kloster Seeon, 10 Mai – 5 Oktober 2008. Seeon: Kloster Seeon, 2008.

Louda, Jiří and Michael Maclagan. *Lines of Succession: Heraldry of the Royal Families of Europe.* London: Orbis Publishing, 1981.

Mead Lalor, William. 'The Grand Duchess Anna Feodorovna: Poor Dear Aunt Julie.' *Royalty Digest: A Journal of Record,* July 1996, 11.

Mead Lalor, William. 'The King Who Loved Beauty: The Story of Ludwig I of Bavaria.' *Royalty Digest: A Journal of Record,* August 1997, 47.

Merten, Klaus. *German Castles and Palaces.* London: Thames and Hudson, 1999.

Millar, Delia. *Views of Germany from the Royal Collection at Windsor Castle: Queen Victoria and Prince Albert on Their Journeys to Coburg and Gotha.* London: The Royal Collection, 1998.

Misniks, Christian. *Hohenschwangau Castle.* Oberammergau: Linderbichl, 2005.

Nelson, Walter Henry. *The Soldier Kings: The House of Hohenzollern*. London: J.M. Dent and sons, 1971.

Oppel, Max. *Schloss Berchtesgaden*. Munich: Hirmer Verlag, 2001.

Prinz von Bayern, Luitpold. *Die Wittelsbacher: Ein Jahrtausend in Bildern.* München: Volk Verlag München, 2014.

Quennell, Peter. *Caroline of England: an Augustan Portrait*. London: Collins, 1939.

Schad, Martha. *Ludwig II*. Munich: dtv, 2016.

Schencks Castles and Gardens: Historic Houses and Heritage Sights. Hamburg: Schenck Verlag, 2012.

Schenk Gräfin von Stauffenberg, Monika and Rainer Benker. *Schloss Greifenstein: Die Grafen Schenk von Stauffenberg.* Berlin: Verlag Monumente und Menschen.

Schinzel Isabella and Eric-Oliver Mader. *Nymphenburg Palace: Pleasure Palace of the Wittelsbachs*. Hamburg: TopSpot Guide.

Schloss Fürstenried: Exerzitienhaus der Erzdiözese München und Freising. Lindenberg: Kunstverlag Josef Fink, 2011.

Schmid, Elmar D. (Edited by). *Die Roseninsel im Starnberger See*. Munich: Bayerische Verwaltung Der Staatlichen Schlösser Gärten und Seen, 2011.

Schmid, Elmar D. and Gerhard Hojer (Edited by). *Linderhof Palace*. Munich: Bayerische Verwaltung Der Staatlichen Schlösser Gärten und Seen, 2006.

Schmid, Elmar D. and Kerstin Knirr (Edited by). *Herrenchiemsee*. Munich: Bayerische Verwaltung Der Staatlichen Schlösser Gärten und Seen, 2007.

Schöber, Ulrike. *Castles and Palaces of Europe*. Lisse: Rebo International, 2006.

Sotnick, Richard. *The Coburg Conspiracy: Victoria and Albert – Royal Plots and Manoeuvres*. Ephesus Publishing, 2008.

Stevens, John (Captain). *The Lives and Actions of all the Sovereigns of Bavaria, kings, dukes, and electors; From the First Erecting that Country into an Absolute State to the Present Year 1706*. London: Printed for J. Morphew, 1706. Gale: ECCO (Eighteenth Century Collections Online Print Editions).

Störkel, Arno. *Christian Friedrich Karl Alexander Der Letzte Margrave von Ansbach-Bayreuth*. Ansbach: Wiedfeld & Mehl: 1995.

Styra, Peter. *Das Haus Thurn und Taxis: Gesamtgeschichte mit Stammfolge*. Werle (Westphalen): Borde Verlag Werl, 2016.

Thornton, Richard. 'Prince Albert's sister and other shady Coburgs.' *Royalty Digest Quarterly*. Falkoping (Sweden): Rosvall Royal Books, 2008 volume 2, 39.

Thurn und Taxis, Princess Mariae Gloria and Todd Eberle. *House of Thurn und Taxis*. New York: Skira Rizzoli, 2015.

Thurn und Taxis, Princess Mariae Gloria and Peter Styra. *Prince Thurn und Taxis Museums Regensburg*. Regensburg: Prince Thurn und Taxis Museums, 2012.

Time to Travel: Travel in Time to Germany's Finest Stately Homes, Gardens, Castles, Abbeys and Roman Remains. Regensburg: Schnell and Steiner, 2010.

Van der Kiste, John. *King George II and Queen Caroline.* Stroud: Sutton Publishing, 1997.

Victoria, Queen of Great Britain and Ireland. *Queen Victoria's Journals: www. queenvictoriasjournals.org.* Windsor: The Royal Archives: 2012.

Von Freeden, Max H. *Schloss Weissenstein in Pommersfelden.* Königstein im Taunus: Verlag Langewiesche.

Von Hagenow, Elisabeth, Luitgard Löw and Andreas von Majewski (Edited by). *Museum of the Bavarian Kings Hohenschwangau: Catalogue on Behalf of the Wittelsbacher Ausgleichsfonds.*

Weschenfelder, Klaus. *Art Collections Veste Coburg.* Regensburg: Schnell &Steiner, 2008.

Wilson, Peter H. *The Holy Roman Empire: A Thousand Years of Europe's History.* Allen Lane, 2016.

Zeepvat, Charlotte. 'The Queen and Uncle E.' *Royalty Digest: A Journal of Record*, July 2000, 2.

Zeune, Joachim. *Castles and Palaces: Germany.* Regensburg: Schmidt Verlag, 2004.

Zeune, Joachim. *Das Hohes Schloss in Füssen.* Regensburg: Schnell & Steiner, 2010.

THE SCHLOSS SERIES OF BOOKS

Schloss is the German word for castle or palace, and you are never far from one of these in Germany. For most of its history Germany was not a single country but a patchwork of royal states, held together under the banner of the Holy Roman Empire. The dukes and princes who ruled these states were passionate builders. Their beautiful castles and palaces, and their compelling personal stories, provide the material for the *Schloss* series of books.

This book can be seen as an inspiration ... to get out there and find the lesser known palaces and learn more about their history. Royalty Digest Quarterly Journal.

Each of the *Schloss* books includes twenty-five beautiful castles and palaces in Germany and looks at these from two perspectives. The first is the author's experience as an overseas visitor to each schloss; the second, colourful stories of the historical royal families connected with them. Royalty have always been the celebrities of their day, and these stories from history can rival anything in modern-day television soap operas.

The second volume is as good as the first, maybe even better – a must... Amazon review.

THE SCHLOSS SERIES OF BOOKS

The stories in the *Schloss* books include the mistress of the king who tried to blackmail him and was imprisoned for forty-nine years; the princess from a tiny German state who used her body and her brains to become the ruler of the vast Russian empire; the prince who defied his family to marry a pharmacist's daughter and then bought her the rank of royal princess; and the duke whose personal story is so colourful he has been called the Bavarian Henry VIII!

Susan Symons has done another fantastic job, proving the point that history can also be fun...
The European Royal History Journal.

The German princes abdicated in 1918, at the end of World War I, and Germany became a republic. As they lost their royal families, many castles and palaces went into decline and became prisons, workhouses, and other institutions. Some were damaged or destroyed in World War II; others lay behind the Iron Curtain for fifty years. The books chart these difficult years and their resurgence and use today as public buildings, museums, and hotels.

The latest addition visits Bavaria – and what a treat it is. Fascinating reading!
The European Royal History Journal

THE SCHLOSS SERIES OF BOOKS

The castles and palaces in the books range in time from fortified castles of the middle-ages; to grand palaces built in imitation of Louis XIV's Versailles; to stately homes from the turn of the early twentieth century. Many are not well known outside Germany and some rarely see an English-speaking visitor. The *Schloss* books might encourage you to go and see these wonderful places for yourself.

The books are sympathetic to our fascinating German royal history and make linkages and connections in a clear and interesting way.
European Castles Institute, Schloss Philippsburg, Germany.

The *Schloss* books are intended to be light-hearted and easy to read. Illustrated throughout and supplemented with charts and family trees, they should appeal to anyone who likes history or sightseeing or is interested in people's personal stories. With dozens of royal families in Germany before the monarchy fell, there are still many more castles and palaces to go, and Susan is already at work on the next book.

This is a well-written, entertaining display of the castles ... I am definitely off to Thuringia, Symons' book in hand.
Royalty Digest Quarterly Journal

SCHLOSS WURZACH
A JERSEY CHILD INTERNED BY HITLER
– GLORIA'S STORY

In the early hours of 16 September 1942 there was a knock on the door of ten-year-old Gloria Webber's home in Jersey. Gloria, her parents and four younger children were all on a list of Jersey civilians to be

deported to Germany on the direct orders of Hitler. Gloria and her siblings, with hundreds of other Jersey children, spent the next years of their childhood interned in an old castle in the south of Germany, called Schloss Wurzach.

Schloss Wurzach was a grand baroque palace built in the eighteenth century by one of Germany's noble families. But by World War II it had fallen on hard times and was used as a prison camp. The schloss was cold, damp, in poor condition, and very

dirty. The internees were horrified by what they found. Twelve of the islanders died in Wurzach during their detention and are buried in the town; others suffered fractured lives.

This short book recalls Gloria's childhood experience and is illustrated with vivid pictures of camp life painted by her father during their confinement. It also describes how she and other internees returned to Germany in later life to celebrate their liberation with the people of Wurzach, showing there can be reconciliation and friendship between former enemies.

Queen Victoria is the monarch from history that everyone knows. These three books focus on the Queen as a woman – her personal life, events that formed her resolute character, and relationships that were important to her. They use some of her own words from her journal, to help tell the story; and are illustrated with portraits and memorabilia from the author's own collection.

Victoria has a life story full of drama, intrigue and surprises. *Young Victoria* covers the bizarre events of her birth, with a scramble to produce the heir to the throne; her lonely childhood under a tough regime; and how she came to the throne at 18.

Victoria & Albert is the story of her marriage to Albert and how she balanced the roles of monarch and Victorian wife and mother. *The Widowed Queen* covers the long years of her life alone after Albert's early death, when she became an icon of the age; the longest serving European sovereign; and matriarch of a huge clan.

Printed in Great Britain
by Amazon

74531125R00136